Harnessing Your True Power to Move Mountains

Move Mountains Initiative Workbook

BY

Janet Wittenauer

WITH CONTRIBUTING AUTHORS
JOAN PRENGER
KEVIN W. COURINGTON
SUZANNE TIPTON OFFNER

BASED ON
THE PHILOSOPHY OF
EXACTLYRIGHT™

www.MoveMountainsInitiative.com

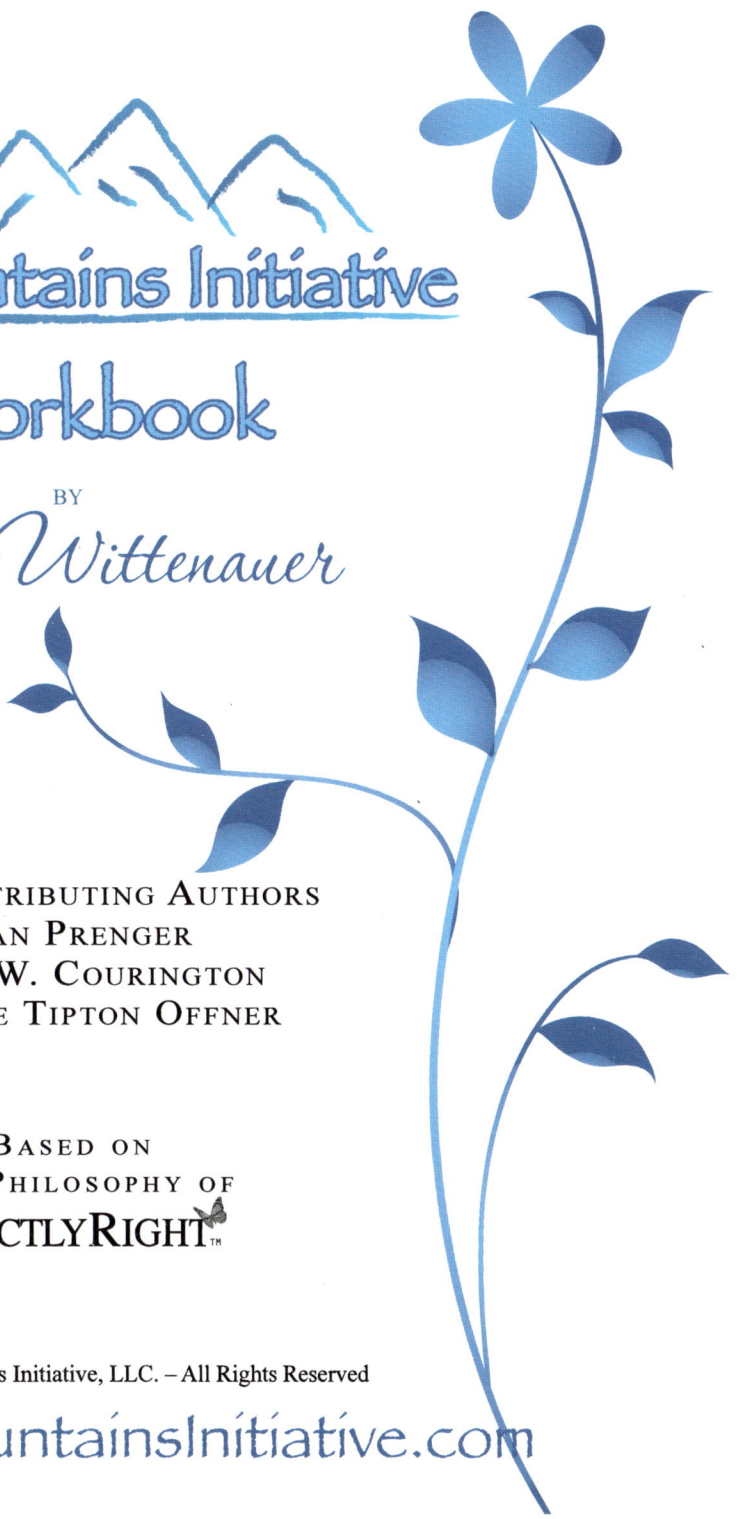

Table Of Contents

Stand In Your Light

By Janet Wittenauer

When I express from the heart
I am who I am
God in action!

I'm connected and present
fully engaged
everything flows...

My true humanity is revealed
I speak my truth
You get my best.

Stand in your light!
Where there is light
there cannot be darkness.

Preface

A few years ago, I was soul-searching for the inspiration that would signal and represent a new chapter in my life's work. I've always believed God has a unique plan for each and every one of us. And I felt ready for a good-sized step that would take me more consciously in that direction. So as I sat in meditation that day, having asked God for guidance and inspiration, the words came through: *Move Mountains Initiative*. I can't say I knew at the time what that meant, but the name resonated within me just the same. So for the past several years I have contemplated, developed and refined this concept. Now I am very pleased to present to you this workbook. It represents step one of Move Mountains Initiative: *harnessing your true power to move mountains*.

As the concept of Move Mountains Initiative began to unfold within me, things started appearing in my life to keep me moving forward. It was as though the universe was actively guiding me toward something wonderful. Then, one day about three years ago, I had the good fortune to meet with a small group of writers who were also on the path of discovery. Kevin Courington, Joan Prenger, and Suzanne Tipton Offner were in the process of writing a book that expressed a philosophy and process for living one's *Exactly Right Life*. After reading their initial draft, what they had to say fit like a glove with my personal philosophy. It seemed to offer the perfect framework for helping people move their personal mountain so that they could re-discover their True Self and design a life that allows that Self to flourish. After much discussion, Kevin, Joan and Suzanne agreed to work with me to expand on the key principles and create an in-depth guide for both new travelers and those who have been journeying a while. We envisioned a thought-provoking, heart-engaging process that is inviting and effective for people ready to make some key changes for the better in their lives. Something that will let your passionate heart come out and play so that you may better remember who you are and why you are here.

Those of you who have already begun your journey will likely recognize the amazing phenomenon that occurred in the writing of this book. Every time we decided to write a chapter, the universe collaborated so that we had to first experience and live it for ourselves before the words finally made it onto the page. We learned first-hand the power and value of putting what we were creating into practice – as we are asking you to do. We learned the blessing of connection as we intentionally called upon each other and the light of Spirit to lead us in the best way – as individuals and as a group. Then we dug deeply into our souls and we dusted off our "Big S Selves" to find that kernel of collective (dare I say universal?) truth for living a life in which mountains no longer present impossible obstacles. Lives in which we get to climb to the top and see all the beauty that the mountaintop offers.

So for this initial step of Move Mountains Initiative, the *Exactly Right* philosophy serves as the foundation for individuals to move their personal mountain—by aligning with their inner greatness and designing their life to reflect and thrive in this greatness. May your journey be filled with discovery, joy and renewed passion for sharing your gifts and your light with the world. God speed!

Introduction

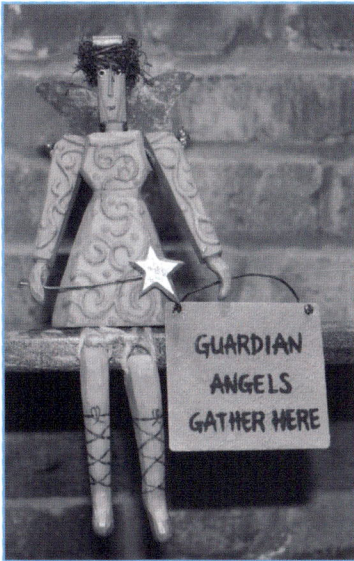

This workbook is meant to take you deeply into yourself. The exercises and explorations will lovingly and, at times, humorously guide you through what can sometimes be a daunting task: knowing, understanding, and appreciating the *Design of You*. This self-knowledge is a key ingredient in creating your own *Exactly Right Life*, and I say it is incredibly worthwhile. Why? Because, to give yourself over to your dreams, and surrender to the beauty of life, you must first know what you have to offer. You must understand and acknowledge the gift that you are before you can share that gift with the world, or even yourself. And finally, the process of learning also, necessarily, includes the process of forgiving, embracing, and loving who you are. The value of this needs no explanation. This workbook is your playground for self-discovery.

The Move Mountains Workbook is, ultimately, an in-depth guide to help you discover and align with your own unique design. It provides opportunities to experiment, play, and dig deeper until you can hear your heart speaking to you. And I encourage you to accept the invitation to play. Yes this subject is important, but it is not required to be "Serious." As one of our mentors once put it: "The Work you must do, but the Struggle is optional!"

For those who like to know up-front what's coming, this workbook has a number of specific purposes built into its design. These purposes include supporting you in listening to your heart and to Spirit as you:

◆ Assess where you are in the process of living your *Exactly Right Life*

◆ Become consciously aware of how you're experiencing your life – right now

◆ Clarify how you want to live your life and have it work for you

◆ Remove the obstacles that are holding you back

- ✦ Connect to your inner calling, and do what you've been dreaming of

- ✦ Put your unique design into action

Give yourself permission to spend the time needed to step through this workbook at a steady pace. If you are working with a group, be sure you get together regularly. Select a quiet peaceful setting that will inspire you and enable you to respond and create from your spiritual core. Let the process unfold naturally.

One final invitation at the outset: Consider working through this with at least one other person that you know and trust. While group work is not required, we found that it enhanced the speed and effectiveness of our understanding. What's more, it gave some accountability to ensure we put all the "good-ideas" into actual practice. Don't underestimate the value of encouragement, feedback and support in this process. It makes burdens lighter and joys brighter.

On that note, I have put together some excellent resources for you on the website: www.MoveMountainsInitiative.com. As you work through the exercises of this workbook, be sure to read and download the Get Mores. They are special tips, audio meditations and additional exercises created by me and my writing team to enhance and expand the ideas of each chapter. In addition, view the blogs and share your wisdom and breakthroughs as you go about experiencing your *Exactly Right Life*. That way, we (the virtual community) can both support you and celebrate your victories.

Dedication

There is an old Zen story about a lion who was brought up by sheep. The lion always thought he was a sheep until an old lion captured him and took him to a pond, where he showed him his own reflection. Many of us are like this lion—the image we have of ourselves comes not from our own direct experience but from the opinions of others. We've become just another sheep in the herd, unable to move freely, and unconscious of our true identity.

I dedicate this workbook to all the lions out there who are ready and willing to wake up, break away from the herd, and claim your special uniqueness. Remember, this is your path. No one can walk it for you. Release the lion within you and live your true destiny. Come with me on a journey of reflection and create your *Exactly Right Life*. Move your mountain! Be who you are designed to be!

Janet Wittenauer

An Exactly Right Life is one you live by choice. It comes from the heart. Rather than living by other people's definition of success, you discover and embrace your own unique design.
You do it in a way that makes you happy and makes your life work, both for you and those around you.

~ Exactly Right Philosophy

What is Exactly Right?

*M*ost of us have a nagging suspicion that there is something better, something more, and something greater that we should be doing with our lives. Yet, we're so busy with life itself, trying to make a living, take care of our loved ones, and be responsible – that we end up cruising through life on autopilot. Even when we do make some progress on our dreams it can be hard to stay motivated and on track. If any of this rings true for you, there is no mistake that you have been led to this workbook.

I am pleased to invite you to take a break from the busyness of life and come with me on a journey of discovery and creation. This workbook will lead you through a practical, yet magical process to design and create your *Exactly Right Life*. This could be the most important journey you'll ever take.

Living the *Exactly Right Life* doesn't mean you do everything right. It doesn't mean that everything works out perfectly, with no hitches and no effort. It means that you are actively choosing to tap into the beauty and magic that is available to you, even in the most ordinary of circumstances. The magic that comes from living the way you were uniquely made.

It's a Funny ✦ Thing ✦

"It's a funny thing about life; if you refuse to accept anything but the best, you very often get it."
~W. Somerset Maugham

You can train yourself to recognize those things that naturally fit with the way you were made to operate. You can live life in a way that flows. You can find a rhythm of life that is as natural as your own heartbeat. It's just that, in the rush to get ahead, we often fail to pay any attention to our hearts. We let stuff get in the way.

At its heart, *Exactly Right* is simply a different way to live. It is learning to be comfortable in your own skin. It's about accessing the things that matter the most to you in your everyday life.

The *Exactly Right* process is loving, challenging, and Spirit-led. It guides you in finding and claiming the truth of who you were uniquely created to be. But it doesn't stop there. It helps you get into action and share your gifts with the world. It helps you connect with others who will support you in sharing your vision and passion. I'll warn you now, it's not always easy. It requires courage and a commitment to making changes in your life that authentically express the *Design of You*. But the payoff is huge.

Trust yourself and your connection to something bigger – to that thing that sources you. You may or may not refer to that thing as "God". You may call it a Higher Power or the Universe or Spirit. I am not writing from the viewpoint of any particular religion. I am not trying to tell you which religion or path to follow. It doesn't matter to me what you call it – only that you call on It as part of this process.

Exercise 1:
How Does It Feel To Be You?

Exactly Right is a very personal process. If you are anything like me, you'll go through your own soul searching and ah-ha moments along the way. Before you can jump into the journey, however, it helps to assess where you are and what's going on for you right now.

Don't be concerned if your mind skips around a lot in the early stages of this process. Self-discovery is like that. It rarely follows neat and orderly patterns. Allow yourself the freedom to do it the way you do it. There is no wrong way.

This workbook is designed with your way in mind. While it has exercises created to take you in important directions, your experience of it will be unique to you. The intent is to give you helpful tools to guide you – tools that will help you assess what your life is like now, and how you want it to be.

Look at the following set of questions. Where are you in each of these areas? Put a check mark where you are now. Put a star where you want to be (not where you "should" be.) Use the first response that comes to mind.

1. Are you clear about your passions?

Not at All	A Little	Halfway	Mostly	All the Way

2. Are you currently living your dreams?

Not at All	A Little	Halfway	Mostly	All the Way

3. Are you doing work that you love?

Not at All	A Little	Halfway	Mostly	All the Way

4. Are you spending time with people that encourage and lift you?

Not at All	A Little	Halfway	Mostly	All the Way

5. Do you feel energized and lively?

Not at All	A Little	Halfway	Mostly	All the Way

6. Do you live in an environment that nourishes and renews you?

Not at All	A Little	Halfway	Mostly	All the Way

7. Are you continually learning and growing?

Not at All	A Little	Halfway	Mostly	All the Way

8. Do you feel connected to Spirit?

Not at All	A Little	Halfway	Mostly	All the Way

9. Are you living the *Exactly Right Life* for you?

| Not at All | A Little | Halfway | Mostly | All the Way |

Maybe the answers you just gave surprised you. Maybe you're all too familiar with your response to some of those questions. Don't worry, wherever you are is just fine. The information in this workbook is designed to help you explore the areas where you want to make some course corrections that will move you forward. It will also help expand and maintain what already works for you. Welcome to *Exactly Right*.

Exercise 2:
Exactly Right/Exactly Wrong

My wish for you is that you reach your highest potential. Here's a great place to start exploring: step back and reflect a minute on the following questions. Don't think it through too much. Just jot down what comes to mind.

1. List the areas of your life that already feel *Exactly Right* for you (i.e. where you feel fulfilled, satisfied, peaceful or inspired).

2. List the areas of your life that feel *Exactly Wrong* for you (i.e. you aren't happy there, you feel stuck, or you're dissatisfied with how things are going).

3. What experiences are missing for your life to feel *Exactly Right*?

For all the areas of your life that already feel *Exactly Right* – rejoice! These are blessings, so just keep going. Pay attention – these areas of your life are a rich source of information about what works for you. Let them nourish your soul.

For the areas where you feel out of balance, frustrated, angry, hurt, or challenged, don't beat yourself up. There's no benefit to self-recrimination. *Exactly Right* works best when you treat yourself with respect and compassion. As frustrating as they may be, these *Exactly Wrong* areas can be your best gifts. They show you where things may be out of balance. They highlight the gap between where you are, and where your heart wants to be. This gap is your chance to explore what your *Exactly Right Life* can look like. If you realize you are out of balance, you can learn what it feels like to be in balance. If you are angry, you can clarify what is unacceptable or unworkable. This gives you a chance to do something about it. An important part of *Exactly Right* is to honor and be grateful for the challenges that show us where to focus our growth. Now is the time to trust yourself and know that you absolutely have what it takes to make the journey into your *Exactly Right Life*.

Self Pledge

I know I am the only one that can give me permission to live the way I was designed.

I pledge to dig in and do the work to have an Exactly Right Life. I give myself permission to create a life I love.

I promise to fully explore and thoroughly enjoy the gift that is me. I intend to get comfortable in my own skin, and love myself the way I am, and the way I'm not.

I will make the most of what I've been given, and share with the world in the best way I know how.

Signed

Date

My Thoughts

_____

_____

_____

_____

_____

_____

_____

_____

_____

_____

_____

_____

_____

_____

_____

_____

_____

As Much As I Dream...

"Only as high as I reach can I grow, only as far as I seek can I go, only as deep as I look can I see, only as much as I dream can I be."

~ Karen Ravn

Welcome to life!
It's messy, it's uncomfortable, it's confusing, and stuff happens. It's also amazing, miraculous, mind blowing, and (let's face it) the only game in town. The real question is, "What do you do in the face of this paradox?"

~ Exactly Right Philosophy

Erase – Focus – Create

So what is involved in living the *Exactly Right Life* for you? It can seem like an overwhelming task. Fortunately, the good news is that you are already perfectly designed. God doesn't create faulty designs. The masterpiece within you already exists. The challenge in creating the *Exactly Right Life* for you is in the discovering and uncovering of the unique *Design of You*.

This exploration process involves three general phases: Erase – Focus – Create. These three phases provide a framework for discovering, acknowledging, and settling into the way you are designed to live. You can approach the exploration process one step at a time, and you can start wherever you like. You can start with your home life, your work life, your spiritual life, any area you feel needs attention. I recommend you start small and work your way up as you gain insight, skills, and confidence.

Genius Is ✦ In All Of Us ✦

"Your spiritual DNA is perfect. It requires no modification or improvement. Genius is in all of us."
~ Bob Proctor

This is not about waving a magic wand and having everything turn out perfect, just the way you thought it should. It's about looking at each situation with new eyes. It's about listening to and following the guidance you receive from your own heart, and from your higher connection. It's about applying the principles of *Exactly Right* with the express purpose of having things work out for you, and everyone around you, better than you could have imagined. As a means to introduce each phase, let's start with the "10,000-foot view". Then later in the book each phase will be discussed in detail, along with how they work.

Erase

When you first imagine your own *Exactly Right Life*, you'll probably come face to face with all the blocks and obstacles that keep you from having it. Don't worry, this is normal. The good news is the vast majority of those obstacles are in your own head. They are outdated beliefs, judgments, habits, and fears that you are holding onto, probably with both hands. Erase is the ongoing process of finding those obstacles and cleaning them out. It's about recognizing and confronting where you sabotage yourself. It's understanding that just because you think something, doesn't mean it's true.

Focus

Once you begin to Erase all the things that have held you back, you create space for your dreams. While we don't often think of empty space as being valuable, it is actually an amazing gift. It is room to be quiet, to listen, and to connect to something much larger than you. This is the space in which you Focus – where you look deep inside and let the truth about who you are come out. This is where you get to know your heart and connect to God – discovering the unique aspects of the *Design of You*.

Your connection to your heart and to God is the most potent guiding force you have. It sheds light on the way you were made to live. It helps you stop second-guessing yourself, and releases you from the trap of what you think you should be. It's in this Focus phase that you learn to stop over-analyzing everything and trying to get it right. You learn how to trust yourself and your gut-feelings. You might even realize that God has a much bigger plan in store for you.

Create

This is the phase where all the preparation, self-discovery and dreaming finally come together. It's where you put your unique design into action. This phase calls for a different kind of action, however. The action of allowing life to happen the way it was meant to be, versus forcing it to bend to your self-limiting expectations. It's actively inviting magic and miracles back into your life. *Create* is somewhat hard to describe but it's amazingly powerful. It's the natural, active expression of all of the time and effort you've invested in the other two phases. And the bolder and more daring you've been in telling the truth about what you want, the more amazing this phase can be. You don't actually make your life *Exactly Right*; you get clear on who you are and let life show up according to that design. You don't chase your dreams; you do your part and let the universe do its part.

Having looked at the 10,000-foot view of *Erase*, *Focus,* and *Create,* let's get a more in-depth, personal introduction to each phase.

Exercise 3:
Erase ~ Any Roadblocks And Unnecessary Negativity

In the *Erase* Phase, you re-evaluate the things that keep you from living your *Exactly Right Life*. These things might be attitudes, actions, relationships, or habits that pull you down versus lift you up. Remember, in this step it is important to look at yourself first, rather than point the finger at others. Then you are accepting responsibility, and therefore acknowledging your power to change the situation.

In your basic nature, you are a pure creation of Spirit. You are perfect just the way you are. Part of that perfection is that you have a dual nature; you are both beauty and the beast. You are loving and spiteful, generous and selfish, tolerant and judgmental. This is just part of the grand design. This idea is captured eloquently in this popular story by an unknown author:

A Native Elder was teaching his grandchildren about life.

He said to them, "A fight is going on inside me. It is a terrible fight, and it is between two wolves. One wolf represents fear, anger, envy, sorrow, regret, greed, arrogance, self-pity, guilt, resentment, inferiority, lies, false pride, superiority, ego, and unfaithfulness.

The other wolf stands for love, joy, peace, hope, sharing, serenity, humility, kindness, forgiveness, benevolence, friendship, empathy, generosity, truth, compassion and faithfulness. This same fight is going on inside you and inside every other person too."

They thought about it for a minute then one child asked his grandfather,
"Which wolf will win?" The Elder simply replied, "The one you feed."

We all have challenges in our lives. Some are real, some are imagined. The "wolf of fear" in each one of us creates all kinds of unnecessary negativity and roadblocks that add to the difficulties of our lives. These products of fear can create toxicity in our relationships, our work, and our own hearts; however, they are built into our design. Our job as humans is to become aware of all aspects of our nature and use each aspect as the gift that it is. Sometimes we need to be angry, so we can see what is not working. Sometimes we need to be selfish, so we can remember to take care of ourselves.

Most of the time, however, we must do the work to feed the "wolf of love". When we treat ourselves with loving compassion, we tend to treat others that way as well. Relationships, businesses, and communities built on openness, compassion, and trust produce a completely different environment than those built on defensiveness, anger, and envy. To build these compassionate communities takes real work, but they are a vital component of living an *Exactly Right Life*. The first step in that work is to clean up the messes we have made by acting out of fear.

In the following chapters you'll go more deeply through the process of Erasing those things that keep you stuck. Before you start to Erase anything, it helps to take stock of what's going on right now. Take a look in your own life – work, home, friendships, family, and communities. Look in your past and your present.

1. In what areas of your life do you listen to the wolf of love?

2. In what ways do you listen to the wolf of fear?

3. What is one simple step you can take this week to create more peacefulness, openness, and healing in one of your relationships, yourself included?

Exercise 4:
Focus ~ On the Heart of the Matter

The *Focus* Phase is where you dig deep into yourself as well as look beyond yourself, to get guidance. You actively seek the inspiration and guidance needed to learn who you are and how you were made to live. As you begin to discover your own unique design, you may also find answers to those issues that have been troubling you.

Focus can be a bit intimidating. It involves your feelings, your emotions, your body responses and your gut instincts far more than your thinking mind. Many of us have much less practice in these non-mental areas.

Facing that intimidation and taking the plunge into Focus will involve trusting yourself. Trusting that deep inside, you know how to live. Trusting that God knows what you need and wants you to know. Ultimately, it's the belief and trust that you will know what's *Exactly Right* for you when you see it and feel it.

So let's begin at the beginning – listening to yourself. The best way I've found to do that is to slow down, create some quiet space, get connected and set the stage for that listening.

One great way to connect is to use this simple meditation I've created called the Heart Level Reflection. Try it and see if it works for you. First read through this entire exercise, and then go through it step by step. Or you can:

✦ Go online to www.MoveMountainsInitiative.com

✦ Click on the Get More tab

✦ Look for the 2.1 Heart Level Reflection post

✦ Download the Heart Level Reflection audio file to hear me personally lead you through this exercise.

Heart Level Reflection

Find a quiet space, free of distractions. Sit either in a lotus position or in a comfortable chair with both feet on the floor, allowing the floor to ground you to the Earth. Try to sit up straight with your spine erect, letting the energy flow smoothly through your body's energy system.

Now, close your eyes and take three deep cleansing breaths. Feel your belly expanding as you slowly breathe in and contracting as you slowly breathe out. With each deep breath, envision yourself breathing in the goodness of Spirit and breathing out all that is weighing on your mind and emotions – your to-do list, worries, concerns, etc. By the end of the third breath, let your mind feel empty.

Take a fourth deep breath and as you breathe in, envision a ball of energy contained in that breath working its way up your spine to the top of your head. And as you breathe out, that ball of energy rolls back down your spine and settles in your heart, becoming bright with light like a rising sun.

Keeping your eyes closed, begin to breath normally again. Stay aware of your breath and stay connected to your heart, basking in the warmth and glow of the light. Relax in this quiet, peaceful place for several minutes, instantly and effortlessly releasing any thoughts or distractions that try to creep into this sacred space. And thoughts will creep in so there's no need to resist them; simply acknowledge them and let them go as if they are floating on by into oblivion. Relax for several minutes feeling the peace emanating from the light.

Now, bring your awareness back to your surroundings. Slowly open your eyes. Thank Spirit for blessing your journey and expanding your awareness.

1. How do you feel now? Describe your experience.

2. What did you learn from this experience?

However you feel now is okay. Sometimes it's easy to slow down and connect, and sometimes it's a challenge. The good news is – it gets easier and more fulfilling with practice.

Exercise 5:
Create ~ Find Your Way To The *Exaclty Right* Outcome

Creating is actively allowing, not just sitting around waiting for things to happen. You take what you have discovered in the Erase and Focus phases and then you begin living according to those discoveries – all the while actively allowing things to turn out *Exactly Right*.

I know it can be difficult to wrap your brain around the concept of consciously expecting and permitting things to turn out *Exactly Right*, so just keep it in the back of your mind as you continue to work through the workbook. This can be a bit confusing, but it will get clearer. It's also where the fun happens.

Now that you have paused and connected, ask yourself, "What do I really want?" "How do I want to live?" Later in this workbook, you'll dig much deeper into creating a life experience that is truly inspiring and workable for you. Before you can begin to create any specifics, it's important to get an overall sense of how you want to experience your life. Do you like things active and fast-paced? Do you value a slower, more methodical speed? Do you work best in a group or by yourself? Look at the list of words on the following page. Which ones jump out at you? Which ones fulfill and inspire you? Set aside your judgments and "shoulds" for this exercise. This is the moment to let your heart sing.

1. Circle the words below that best describe how you want to experience your life.

Abundance	Efficiency	Love	Romance
Achievement	Enough	Magic	Security
Acknowledgment	Excitement	Motivation	Self Expression
Active	Exploration	Natural	Sensitivity
Adventure	Family	Nature	Sensuality
Aliveness	Flow	Newness	Sexiness
Appreciation	Freedom	Organic	Simplicity
Balance	Friendship	Outrageousness	Solitude
Beauty	Fulfillment	Passion	Spirit Led
Calmness	Fun	Peace	Spiritual
Choice	Grace	Play	Steadiness
Community	Growth	Pleasure	Success
Compassion	Happiness	Power	Team
Completeness	Harmony	Productivity	Understanding
Connectedness	Health	Profitability	Vitality
Creativity	Inspired	Relatedness	Winning
Ease	Joy	Relationships	Wonder
Effectiveness	Learning	Rhythm	Workability

Feel free to add some of your own:

2. Pick three to six of your circled words that are most empowering to you when you think of your *Exactly Right Life*:

The words you have chosen here are just one inside glimpse of how you are designed. They begin to express what you know about your unique design as a human being.

You may already be judging the words you picked. You may be trying to pick the right words or impressive words. Don't worry about it. Those judgments are normal – just don't fall into the trap of believing them. The most important thing now is to notice what is actually fulfilling and inspiring to you, versus what you think you should be like.

Exercise 6:
Dream Board

Now it's time to create a Dream Board based on the words you selected above. For those of you who have never done one, a Dream Board is a tool to visually capture the essence of what you are creating – using photos, drawings, pictures, words, colors, symbols, textures – whatever inspires or speaks to you. In creating your board, O Magazine's Martha Beck advises the following: "Just page through a magazine (and walk through the world) noticing things that trigger physical reactions: a heart thump, a double take, a gasp… These 'thoughts' register in your stomach, your heart, your lungs—anywhere but your head." [1]

No artistic skill is required – just express, play, and create. Avoid the temptation to judge the quality of your efforts. You are not looking to get it right. You are just looking for creative expressions that capture the feelings of how you want your life to be. By letting your creativity and passion guide you, you can explore and clarify those things that mean the most to you. When you go back later and look at what you've created, it should conjure up and reignite those feelings all over again.

Use the following blank page provided, or use a large piece of poster-board for this exercise. Here are some ideas for creating your Dream Board:

✦ Find pictures or words in magazines

✦ Choose photos of your own

✦ Use crayons, paints, markers or colored pens

✦ Pick items from nature

✦ Write words in a creative way

✦ Make up your own symbols that represent your ideas

✦ Feel free to color outside the lines. This is mostly about having fun and expressing yourself. Create whatever appeals to you.

---

1. O Magazine, June 2010, The Vision Thing by Martha Beck, pages 43-47.

Dream Board

Later on, you'll explore ways to bring these ideas from your Dream Board to life. As you continue this process, you'll want to refer back to your Dream Board often, to make sure what you are doing lines up with the intentions you created. You can always update this original Dream Board if things change for you. And, over time things will change as you grow. Simply allow your vision to grow as you do.

Get More Free Stuff

More is available!

Additional tools, articles, and recorded meditations have

been created to support your journey.

Check it out at:

www.MoveMountainsInitiative.com

on the Get More tab

For this chapter, look for:

2.1 Heart Level Reflection Audio

My Thoughts

_____
_____
_____
_____
_____
_____
_____
_____
_____
_____
_____
_____
_____
_____
_____
_____

Trust the Joy

"Trust that what brings you joy is leading you somewhere."

~ Kenny Loggins

When we're moving fast
and always doing-doing-doing, we operate like
an airplane on autopilot. We go in one particular
direction and do what we "have to do". Sadly, we
can easily lose sight of our dreams and the things
that make life truly worthwhile.

~ Exactly Right Philosophy

3

Step Back and Breathe

The first phase in living your *Exactly Right Life* is to step back and breathe. Slow down. Choose to step out of the rat race and find a quiet space, even if it is just for a few minutes at a time. It is in this quiet space with a calm and clear mind that you connect to the *Design of You*. This is where your dreams, passions, and "truth" reside. In addition, stepping back allows you to look at your life from a bird's eye view – enabling you to see the bigger picture. You can also see the truth of what's working and what's not working in your life. It gives you the space to question all the assumptions that get in the way of your dreams. In fact, to truly live your *Exactly Right Life*, you'll want to make it a priority to have regular appointments for reflection time.

✦ Get Ready ✦

"Get ready my soul. I'm diving in…"
~ Lyrics by Daniel Nahmod

Exercise 7:
Autopilot vs. Being Engaged

Take a few centering breaths, then reflect on the following questions. They are designed to help you see where you're running on autopilot versus being fully engaged in the moment. Keep the last 30-60 days in mind when doing this exercise.

1. In what instances have you felt fully engaged and plugged into a task, activity, or conversation – where your mind didn't wander and you were able to give it your full attention and energy?

2. Describe how that felt to be fully engaged?

3. Now think about the opposite, where you're running on automatic; unconsciously tackling task after task. Describe how being in autopilot mode feels.

4. What aspects of your life seem to be on autopilot?

5. Now the true gut check! What percentage of your time is spent in autopilot mode? Are you willing to settle for this?

We all have some required tasks that we don't necessarily like to do. But we don't have to put ourselves in autopilot mode to get them done. Creating an *Exactly Right Life* includes finding ways to manage these mundane tasks in a way that fits and flows with our design.

The good news is that we have the ability to create an *Exactly Right Life* where we can be present and totally engaged more often than not. To take ourselves off autopilot, however, we have to recognize our habitual ways of doing things.

6. When life gets hectic, do you take a step back to get calm? If not, why not? What stops you?

7. What do you do to step back, slow down, breathe, and reflect? How often are you doing that?

Exercise 8:
Identify and Create Your Own Personal Retreat

In Chapter 2, you found a place free of distractions and did the Heart Level Reflection. Now, we would like you to go one step further and identify several quiet places – at home, at work, in the neighborhood – where you feel most aware and connected. Think of these places as personal retreats, where you can simply slip away for a short period of time to clear your mind and connect. Some examples include: a library, park, conference room, patio, sunroom, chapel, church, bookstore, garden, woods, or simply a quiet corner in your bedroom.

1. What are (or could be) your personal retreats at home, work, or in your neighborhood?

✦ Home

✦ Work

✦ Neighborhood

You may want to take an extra step and enhance these places to create an even more peaceful environment, adding items such as: candles, spiritual symbols, artwork, inspirational quotes and books, personal journal, meditation music, incense, pictures, and your Dream Board. At the very least, create one quiet place that inspires you.

2. What does it feel like for you to be in your personal retreat?

One of the easiest ways to naturally and quickly get to that place of peace, harmony and connectedness is to be out in nature. Nature teaches us stillness and present-moment living. Eckhart Tolle says it well:

> *"Go out into nature. Use your senses fully and let the alert stillness within you be the perceiver, rather than your mind. When you perceive without thought, you are open to the presence of the Divine."* [1]

Sometimes it is difficult to find a quiet place, especially if you're traveling away from home. Another option is to create that quiet place in your imagination. This option is especially fun because you are free to create the most incredible place you can imagine. Think of the most beautiful place you've ever been in your travels, or the most beautiful nature picture you've seen. You can go there in your imagination. What is the weather like? Where will you sit? What does the landscape look like around you? What nature sounds do you hear? What birds or animals do you see? Do you smell the flowers? All you have to do is close your eyes and you'll be there.

3. Create your imaginary personal retreat. Describe it in detail.

Take time to appreciate the gift of quiet reflection – the time that you have set aside to connect and nurture yourself. It can be a place of inspiration, relaxation, and rejuvenation whenever you need it.

---

1. Eckhart Tolle's Findhorn Retreat: Stillness Amidst The World. DVD. 2006. Owl Productions. New World Library and Eckhart Teachings.

Get More Free Stuff

More is available!

Additional tools, articles, and recorded meditations have

been created to support your journey.

Check it out at:

www.MoveMountainsInitiative.com

on the Get More tab

For this chapter, look for:

3.1 Get Centered: A Simple Prayerful Conversation
3.2 Quick Calming Techniques
3.3 Try Journaling
3.4 Create Your Own Internal Quiet Place

My Thoughts

_____

_____

_____

_____

_____

_____

_____

_____

_____

_____

_____

_____

_____

_____

_____

_____

_____

Free Yourself

"You don't have to control
your thoughts, you just have to
stop letting them control you."
– Dan Millman

We have all created a box that defines
the way we live, what we can and can't do.
For most of us, we are so busy trying to get it all
done that we no longer recognize or question
our boxes. Imagine feeling, dreaming, and
living "outside the box" – or maybe
creating the perfect box for you...

~ Exactly Right Philosophy

4

Do a Reality Check

The personal retreat you've discovered or created in Chapter 3 is the perfect place to take a good long look at your life and do a reality check. Sometimes, when you stop and get quiet, it becomes obvious that certain parts of your life don't work the way that you would like them to. This fact is one of the primary reasons so many of us are reluctant to slow down. We are afraid our lives will catch up to us and we'll have to face the truth. What is surprising, however, is that when you quiet your mind and really reflect, some of the things that you were most afraid of – that felt most like insurmountable problems or roadblocks – suddenly don't seem like such a big deal. With time and room to really look at it, you can often recognize where you are blowing things out of proportion, either by over-emphasizing their importance, or by harshly judging how you are handling them. From a peaceful mindset you can then go to work on life's challenges – the ones, when handled, that will make the most difference.

Welcome the ✦ Unwelcome ✦

"When we welcome what we most want to avoid, we evoke divinity itself."
~ Geneen Roth

Becoming Aware Of Your Story

So much of what we experience is the result of our reaction to the circumstances of life. It's not the circumstances themselves that impact us so much – it is how we interpret them.

We are constantly making up judgments and labels about what happens to us. We don't have a tire blow on the way to work... Instead, "My car hates me and my day is ruined." We don't have a nine-task to-do list… Instead, "I am overwhelmed and have a million things to get done." Some of this is the simple human penchant for drama. The rest is our natural tendency to make up a judgment or label as a reaction to the world around us. Collectively we call these judgments and labels our stories. Some of our stories are inconsequential and harmless, and some of our stories place us in a box. It's a box of our own making that is limiting and uninspiring — and frankly, not the truth of who we really are.

> "I am convinced that life is 10% what happens to me and 90% how I react to it."
>
> ~ Pastor Charles Swindoll

The purpose of this chapter is to help you identify your stories, looking deeply and truthfully within as if you're holding a mirror to your soul. Then, by taking a step back as a non-judgmental observer, you can acknowledge whether your stories are a fit for your life, or not. Do some of the walls of the box you've built for yourself (called your Life) need a bit of re-modeling? What about stretching and dreaming beyond the box? What about creating a box that acknowledges and even enhances your gifts, and honors and manages your weaknesses? By simply becoming aware of your stories, you will naturally be empowered to adjust those judgments and labels to better serve you in creating your *Exactly Right Life*.

Exercise 9:
Label Maker

Let's begin by doing a reality check on the most basic and fundamental story of your life – The story of "Who Am I?" In this exercise we will scratch the surface layers of those labels that you've applied to you and your life. Take a moment to get centered and settled into a quiet space.

Step 1

1. Sit down with a timer and give yourself at least five minutes.

2. In the first column on the next page, write down every label that applies to you or your life (e.g., Latino, Buddhist, single mother, red-head, overweight, etc). Don't edit yourself – just write everything that comes to mind and keep adding to the list till the timer goes off. This is a place for radical honesty. Don't sugar coat it – really be open about what comes up for you.

Step 1 - Label

Step 2 - Judgment

_____

_____

_____

_____

_____

_____

_____

_____

_____

_____

_____

_____

_____

_____

_____

Step 2

1. Now go back and set the timer for another five minutes.

2. In column two on the previous page, evaluate and provide a personal judgment for each of the labels that you wrote. For example, if you wrote "Latino" in the first column for Step 1, then beside it in the column for Step 2, write what that means to you, perhaps "family oriented". Again, do not edit yourself – write down the first judgment of that label that comes to your mind. Below are a few more examples.

Step 1 - Label	Step 2 - Judgment
Latino	Family Oriented
Buddhist	Misunderstood
Single mother	Exhausted
Red-head	Fun
Overweight	Fast Food Junkie

3. Now, look at the lists you made and consider the following questions:

    ✦ What did you learn about your labels and how you judge them?

We have a multitude of Stories for our lives. It is just a natural part of being human. Many of our judgments and labels don't overly affect us one way or the other. However, there are certain ones, good and bad, which stand out for each of us.

4. Which three of your labels or judgments from the exercise most stand out for you?

5. Which three bother you the most and why?

6. Which three are you the proudest of, or would you miss the most if they were taken away?

Sometimes our judgments and labels naturally fall into groups of ideas that are related forming recognizable themes. Those themes often have a much greater impact on the way we experience our lives than just the individual labels. They can form the basis of how we believe life is and who we are supposed to be.

7. From looking at your list, what are the overall themes that stand out for you or your life?

Sometimes it's easier to see stories in others than to see our own. We're so used to our own stories, we're often blind to them. Ask trusted friends or family members to help you. Often times they can quickly identify a few of your labels that stand out to them. Remember to keep an open mind and try not to be judgmental in this process.

Exercise 10:
Early Labels

Now it's time to dig down another layer and look at labels or roles acquired while growing up. This exercise can give you some very valuable insight into your Stories.

1. In my family growing up, I was the _____ one: (Circle any that apply to you, or add your own.)

Bullying	Invisible	Responsible
Busy	Lazy	Serious
Cranky	Lonely	Smart
Crazy	Lost	Solid
Different	Loud	Strong
Dutiful	Mean	Stubborn
Fanciful	Ornery	Stupid
Free Spirited	Outgoing	Thoughtful
Funny	Peacemaking	Ugly
Golden	Plain	Wacky
Gullible	Playful	Weak
Happy	Pretty	Weird
Insecure	Quiet	Wild

The role we play early on often becomes the Story of our life. Sometimes we stick with it because it's more comfortable. Sometimes it's just a good fit for our personalities. And sometimes we become attached to our role, because it doesn't feel safe or okay to do something else. It becomes who we think we are and all we know.

2. Which roles are still very prevalent within your life?

3. Which roles have you let go?

4. Which roles would you like to let go?

It can take some time to truly identify the underlying themes and roles that compose the Stories of our lives. Journaling is a very useful tool for jotting down labels and stories that you notice in your conversations and self-talk during the course of a day. Over time, as you accumulate a fair number of them, you'll more clearly see the themes. Becoming aware of your Stories is the first key step in doing your reality check. Now, let's go to the second step.

Separating Yourself From Your Story

We are so much more than our stories. You have begun to see that stories make up the walls of the box we've built for ourselves, this box called Life. In doing a reality check you begin to question, "Are these walls limiting me or supporting me? Do they reflect my personal integrity and what I value most in life? Or, do they represent what I think I should do, rather than what's in my heart to do?" A box built of shoulds often shows up looking like you have no choice – "That's just the way it is!" Now is the time to break the chains of shoulds!

One of the most effective ways I've found to re-model the walls and change your experience of life is to locate the source of that experience – your Story. Then you can rewrite it. This process is called Re-Storying. It's a powerful step towards living the *Exactly Right Life* for you.

Before you can Re-Story your life, however, you must first separate your stories into their two most basic parts – What Happened and Interpretation:

✦ What Happened consists of just the facts, the important objective circumstances of the story. Things like, "He told me, I don't like how you did this report," or "He hit the ball through my car window."

✦ Interpretation consists of judgments, opinions and embellishments of those facts. For example "He told me my work sucked and then went ballistic." or "That kid tried to destroy my new car!" Did you catch the extra dramatic elements in the Interpretation part?

If you take a step back as a non-judgmental observer, you'll see it is rarely What Happened that causes us grief. It is our Interpretations that make things difficult to deal with. As humans we get invested in the Interpretation of our stories, because it lets us put a spin on events that serves our needs. Sometimes we want to appear like the victim, sometimes we want to appear the hero. We can tell the story any way that suits us. So the real question is, how do we create a story that really works for us – one that makes our heart sing?

Exercise 11:
A Deeper Look at Your Stories

Imagine that our labels and Stories are like a closet full of coats. They are all different shapes, sizes and colors. Each coat represents a different way to tell your story. We have the option to pick any coat in the closet. We can grab the dowdy brown one ("I'm not really that smart. People don't care what I say.") Or we can try on the zebra striped coat ("I may be quiet, but when I talk it's usually worthwhile!") The point is, we can try them on, and take them off. We can create explanations for what happens to us. Why create explanations that are disempowering? How about we choose the coat that makes us feel great and helps us be more effective?

Try on some of the coats in your closet and see how they feel.

1. Think of a story in your life that is upsetting to you. You may choose one of the ones you've identified in the previous exercises, or pick a new one. This exercise is more powerful if you choose something that matters to you. What is really on your mind? You can write down the basics of that situation here:

2. Now take a step back, and look at your Story from a new perspective. Let's identify the pieces of your Story. Is there a villain? Is there a victim? Are there any heroes? Is it a love story? An adventure? A comedy? A drama? A comic tragedy?

3. How do you explain what happened in your Story? Why are things the way they are? For example: "People always call me because I'm the only one who can get it done right", "I'll never be wealthy because I'm cursed around money", or "I'll never exercise and lose weight because I have no willpower." Don't try and sound enlightened here. Be honest – see if you can pinpoint what you really think about your situation. Use one or more of the following starter phrases to write a brief explanation of your story below: This happened because...; It is this way because...; I know this is true because...; Things will never change because...

_____

_____

_____

_____

Now, here's the tough part. Consider that the explanations you gave aren't true. Of course they feel true. And your feelings are real. They're just not the whole story. If you think about it, you really don't know why something happened. Only that it did happen.

For example: "I always overeat, because I have no willpower." If that is your Story, it probably feels like the truth to you. And because it feels like the truth, you will often argue and fight to prove it. But if you look deeper, most likely you'll find many examples that confirm that you do have willpower. After all, it is required for any kind of accomplishment. The question is, are you willing to do what it takes to honor and recognize the willpower you do have, and look at why you aren't applying it with food? That's very different than, "I have no willpower."

So what if there is another explanation that is just as valid? And what if that explanation is more empowering to you? Wouldn't it be more fun and less stressful to operate from a less dramatic version of events? For instance, a new version might be "I've been overeating because my weight helps me hide from people. But I am conquering my fear of being seen by people. I don't need to hide anymore." I am not suggesting you stick your head in the sand and ignore legitimate problems. But it is important not to assign negative motives where they don't belong. If this seems difficult, remember to step back and be the non-judgmental observer of your own life. Get some help from a wise friend or mentor if you need it.

✦ *The Ups and Downs of Stories* ✦

An important thing to remember is there are ups and downs to our Stories. Some of our Stories tell us who to be and what to do, for example, "I'm charming and people like me." The upside to having this Story is, you're most likely to be confident and feel very comfortable when you meet new people.

The downside to any Story is when you get so locked into it that you allow it to restrict your choices. For instance, if your Story is "I'm the happy person, always ready with a smile," are you allowed to ever have a bad day? If you are strong, are you allowed to ask for help? Instead of being inspiring, sometimes being the bread-winner becomes, "I have no choice but to work like a maniac." And if you can no longer fulfill your role as the breadwinner, do you lose all self esteem? That is why it is important to separate yourself from your Story. Give yourself room to see new interpretations of old facts.

In *Exactly Right*, you have the freedom to be creative, expressive and to be yourself – and you grant that freedom to others. This doesn't mean spinning naïve fairy tales that are all sweetness and light. It means being intentional and thoughtful about how we decide to tell a story, even to ourselves. It means taking responsibility for our own actions, knowing that it is the road to freedom. It means telling the story that works for you and everyone around you.

Once you recognize just how much your life experiences are influenced by your Stories, you will better understand why you feel stuck in certain areas of your life. Armed with this understanding, you can recreate the Story of your life in a new and supportive way, a way that can be *Exactly Right* for you.

Rewriting Your Story

I hope you got a sense that how you tell your Story greatly impacts your feelings and your ability to act. Your experience changes with how you explain the events. I have found that the best stories aren't made up at all. They are discovered, uncovered, or revealed. Your best story is one from your heart.

Exercise 12:
Designing A New Story From Your Heart

You were made in a particular way, with your own special talents, gifts, desires, and dreams. In the world of *Exactly Right* the unique *Design of You* is written on your heart by Spirit. This is who you are. This is what you were made to do. This is your special gift.

What if the Story you told about yourself is, "I have something to offer that no one else ever could"? And what if the Story you told is, "My gift is the perfect thing to give to the world"? How would you act then?

1. What attributes are you proud of (e.g. I'm a natural writer. I'm a good organizer. I'm good with kids. I love to work with my hands. Math comes easily to me.)? What have others complimented you on? These are good indicators of your natural gifts. List them here. Now is not the time to be shy or modest.

2. What do you love to do? What inspires and excites you? (e.g. I enjoy personal growth courses. I love to spend time with kids. I'm passionate about new technology. My greatest joy is nurturing my garden.) What do you spend your time doing, even when you should be doing other things? What are those things you do at the drop of a hat? Nobody has to twist your arm to do these things. You love to talk about them. List them here.

3. Some experiences in our lives support us and lift us up. They feed us. You could even call them nutritional experiences, because we feel stronger and more complete when we do them (e.g. playing with your kids, attending a spiritual service, doing yoga, snuggling, sailing, singing, praying.) They help you connect to your source and fulfill you. What are those experiences for you?

4. Some of us have passions and dreams that we've yet to express. Perhaps they seem too big or out of reach. Maybe they live only in our imaginations. Now is the time to trust that they are there for a reason. What have you been secretly wishing and hoping for?

5. What do you need to feel safe and secure? What are the things that you just can't do without? (e.g. I have to have my checkbook balanced. I need to know my partner loves me. I need some down time. I have to be up on current events. I have to look my best.) These are the non-negotiable items that you know you need in place. They are different for every person. What are yours?

6. Look back at what you've just written in questions 1-5. This is a good start in understanding the unique *Design of You*. Take a moment and summarize your responses on the following page. Or, grab a blank piece of paper and write an empowering and inspiring Story that captures the design of your *Exactly Right Life*.

The Design of Me

✦ I am a special and unique person. My natural gifts are:

✦ I am inspired and excited when I'm:

✦ The nutritional experiences that truly feed my soul and make me strong include:

✦ Deep down, I have secretly been longing to do:

✦ For my life to work best, the things that I just can't do without include:

By understanding yourself and how you are designed, you can create new and empowering Stories that fit that design. For instance, instead of hating your flightiness and forgetfulness, you might honor your free spirit and insightfulness. Instead of regretting your stubbornness, you might appreciate your faithfulness. Our strengths and weaknesses are an essential part of who we are. Allow your best to come forward. By telling a Story in a way that celebrates your nature, you can deal with the upsides and the downsides more effectively.

In short, Re-Storying is making yourself the hero of your own Story, and allowing others to be the hero of theirs. What an awesome and freeing way to participate in life.

Get More Free Stuff

More is available!

Additional tools, articles, and recorded meditations have

been created to support your journey. Check it out at:

www.MoveMountainsInitiative.com

on the Get More tab

4.1 The "If You Say So" Game

4.2 Who Am I?

4.3 Crazy Stories We Tell

4.4 Dealing With The "Sacred Cow" Stories of Life

4.5 The Pain of Believing the Stories We Tell

4.6 Declaring Miracles

4.7 Living in Pronoia

4.8 The Power of Radical Honesty

My Thoughts

_____

_____

_____

_____

_____

_____

_____

_____

_____

_____

_____

_____

_____

_____

_____

_____

Attracting Success

"Success is not to be pursued;
it is to be attracted by the
person you become."

~ Jim Rohn

As you grow in your ability to deal powerfully with those Exactly Wrong moments, you become someone whose dreams are no longer permanently thwarted by life's twists and turns. And in the process, you can finally break through the walls that have kept you from your Exactly Right Life.

~ Exactly Right Philosophy

Lighten the Load

$\mathcal{L}$ife happens! Sometimes things just don't go the way we think they should. Sometimes people we love let us down. Sometimes the pressures of life reach the boiling point and things just feel *Exactly Wrong*. How we deal with these disappointments, upsets and painful experiences often determines whether or not they stick with us and become our defining labels and stories. From the previous chapter, it's clear that not all labels and stories are harmful. However, many of those we carry with us are less than empowering. Over time, they become like a bag of rocks in our backpacks, acting as barriers to living our *Exactly Right Life*. How do we stop accumulating the rocks? Better yet, how do we eliminate the entire bag of rocks on our backs?

In this chapter you will work on lightening your load. You'll get to revisit and let go of the old baggage of hurts and disappointments, expectations, limiting beliefs, self-doubt, and the addiction to external approval. Learning to let go will open up even more space for your *Exactly Right Life* to shine through.

The Gift
✦ of Troubles ✦

"Troubles are often the tools by which God fashions us for better things."
~ Henry Ward Beecher

Looking For The Gold

Consider that everything that's ever happened to you is an essential ingredient that you needed to be able to get where you are. And consider that you needed to get here in order to do that thing that you were designed for – to share your unique gifts and passions with the world. Each experience we have, whether good or seemingly not-so-good, is meant to guide us or teach us. Each circumstance that happens contains a valuable lesson. So it's important to look closely at each experience with an explorer's eye and harvest the lesson meant specifically for you. It's also important to listen to your heart as you look for the lesson so that you see how it fits into the overall plan. In this way, you can integrate the valuable parts of any circumstances into your *Exactly Right Life*.

Looking for the lessons life is sending you every day helps combat what I call the Cosmic "Two-By-Four" Syndrome. That's where the universe is trying to tell you something so a particular circumstance or event will occur in your life. Often it comes to you subtly, but enough to get your attention if you let it. If you ignore the message, however, life sends a little stronger version – less easy to ignore. If you are really resistant to the message then the universe smacks you with a cosmic two-by-four circumstance to get your attention. The goal here is to get the lesson before you get to the two-by-four stage.

But once you get the lesson, you must go further and let go of the circumstances that brought the lesson to you. Consciously let go of the upset, hurt, disappointment, guilt or other feelings that accompanied the lesson.

> "The Universe is willing to teach us with the tickle of a feather if we would just listen. Otherwise, wait long enough and you'll get a sledgehammer."
>
> ~ Gay Hendricks

✦ *Kevin's Story* ✦

When I lost my father a couple of years ago, one of the great lessons I learned from his death was not to put my life on hold for "someday".

My father always intended to travel once he retired but he kept putting it off. Unfortunately, shortly after his retirement, cancer took over his body and any opportunity to travel was lost.

His death was certainly a two-by-four moment for me. I, too, kept putting off things I've always wanted to do. One of the things I had put off was some opportunities to fly down and see Dad. He lived several states away and it just never seemed the right time or the right financial situation to fly down.

Luckily, I did go down for a couple of weeks before his death. But I had almost waited until it was too late. And despite our time together, I kept thinking "If only I would have come to visit more often!"

It took his death for me to get the lesson. There were many other areas of my life waiting for "someday." Once I got through the pain and the loss, along with some guilt, I discovered what a valuable gift he had left me; someday is now!

Often, letting go will involve forgiving yourself or someone else before you can fully release it. It may also take some time to just be with the totality of the event and separate its pieces so that you can release the parts that don't help you. Regardless, getting the lesson often means spending time releasing and letting go of emotions and attachments to the events themselves and looking at them from a one-step-removed viewpoint.

Personally, I have found that the following steps can assist you in the process of releasing attachments, letting go of hurt and resentment, and finding freedom in forgiveness:

Step 1: **Be with it.** Sit still for a moment, set aside any judgments, and just allow the experience to be exactly like it is. Be brave enough to allow yourself to fully feel any emotion that is there. Don't run away from it – relax and let yourself experience fully. Finally, just let all those emotions go. Let them fall away so that you are not stopped by them anymore. Once you can be with the situation, you may choose to go further and replay what happened with a detective's eye. Courageously notice the source of the pain, guilt, upset or discomfort. Who else was involved? How did you respond? How did the other person(s) respond? What were the consequences of your actions and theirs?

Step 2: **Pan for gold.** From the observer mode you can look for the golden nuggets – the lessons. You probably noticed some things you didn't see before. What did this teach you? What will you take away from it? As you face the truth of the experience, looking at it with an open heart, you begin to see the lessons as blessings, moving you ever forward on your journey.

> "When you get into a tight place and it seems that you can't go on, hold on—for that's just the place and the time that the tide will turn."
> ~ Harriet Beecher Stowe

Step 3: Forgive, then let it go. This is an important step to allow for the pain and upset to be fully released. Forgiveness doesn't have to be complicated. Forgiveness is for you, for allowing the release of any negative energy you've been clinging to and getting things flowing again. It is this flow which will remove blockages, make room in your life for new opportunities, and bring into your life the new things you need to grow.

Note that I am not trying to downplay, or ask you to condone cruel and malicious behavior on the part of others. In most situations, however, you will find that the other person wasn't intentionally trying to scar you for life. They may have acted through ignorance or out of their own pain, unaware of its effect on you. You may also realize that your response to the situation wasn't as loving or "enlightened" as you know you're capable of either. This is not the time to crucify yourself or others on the tree of "I should have" or "He shouldn't have."

> "Forgiveness is the finishing of old business that allows us to experience the present, free of contamination from the past."
> ~ Joan Borysenko

Sometimes the best solution is to harvest the lesson and set the rest aside. I encourage you to try the Letting Go Meditation in the following exercise.

Exercise 13:
A Letting Go Meditation

Because forgiveness and letting go are so powerful and beneficial to living the *Exactly Right Life,* I have created a Letting Go Meditation to assist you. It will lead you on a very visual and peaceful journey to forgive and let go of events and emotions that have kept you upset and stuck. You may want to download it and use it when you feel a need to forgive and lighten the load. It is my gift to you. You'll find it at:

www.MoveMountainsInitiative.com

Click on the Get More tab
Look for 5.1 Letting Go Meditation

Dismantling The Box Built Of Shoulds

So often, when we begin to look at our lives in an effort to improve them, we start criticizing what we see. We start noticing all of those things we don't like and that seem out of place. We start comparing those things to what we think they "should be." We look at our lives and notice, often for the first time, the box we've built for ourselves and we get discouraged.

The box we've created defines the way we live, what we can and can't do. It defines the hopes and dreams we are allowed to have and those we have to put on the shelf because they are not okay. It determines the acceptable way we should live and the things about us that are off limits. We are not usually present to that box until it's pointed out to us, or until we decide to take a look at ourselves in an effort to make a change. Once we become present to our boxes, we often feel constrained or locked into them. We see everything about them that's wrong, and we immediately want to find a way to break the boxes down.

In this section, I encourage you to come at it differently. In this phase, I invite you to notice your own box, but not to immediately set about dismantling it. First, spend some time really studying it. Don't be surprised if you don't like what you find. But, allow yourself to see the useful parts too — look for which walls work for you and which don't.

As human beings, we need limits and boundaries to manage the overwhelming number of choices, options and possibilities that come our way every day. We have to have some way of figuring out what to do. We create boxes for ourselves to keep from being overwhelmed. We use the walls to help us navigate and function.

The key is to let go of all of the walls that are built out of "shoulds" and instead choose ones designed to support you. You choose which self-imposed limitations support your integrity and personal responsibility. Not what you "should do," but what you were made to do. What your heart is telling you that you were designed for.

Exercise 14:
Your Own Battle of Jericho

In the Biblical story of the Battle of Jericho, God delivered the city of Jericho into the hands of Joshua and the Children of Israel by bringing down the seemingly unbreakable walls. What seemed like an overwhelming obstacle was swept away to make way for victory.

In our own lives it seems like we often face insurmountable walls that lock us in or keep us away from the lives we want. If only we could just sweep those walls away… Of course, as I have already mentioned, not all our walls are bad. How can we topple the ones that don't work while keeping the ones that do work? One great way to start is to put the issue into the hands of Spirit and see where that takes you.

My friend and contributing author, Kevin Courington, has created an audio visualization exercise to let you begin dismantling your unwanted walls. He uses the walls of Jericho as an analogy for tearing down your own blocks and barriers.

Go to the website at:

www.MoveMountainsInitiative.com

Click on the Get More tab
Look for 5.2 The Jericho Exercise

Embracing Our Flaws

If there is anything more insidious than the conflicting external messages of what we should and shouldn't do, it is the unreasonable expectations of who we think we should and shouldn't be. When most of us assess our lives, the greatest part of what we see is a motley collection of flaws, inadequacies, weaknesses and failings we believe we have. This collection of flaws seems to scream out all the reasons why we are not up to the task of having the lives we want. It's almost as if, now that we look at it, we can understand why such a flawed person would have, maybe even deserve, such a flawed life. Okay, maybe that's a bit melodramatic but so many people behave as if they are stuck with unacceptable lives and have no choice.

I believe this sense of fatalism comes from at least two sources: First, we find many more "flaws" in ourselves than are actually there due to our incessant drive to unreasonably compare ourselves to other people. Second, we believe that any flaw we see is necessarily "bad" – a liability that must be overcome or covered up if we are to have any hope at all. These two sources can form a trap that can seem insurmountable.

> "If you hear a voice within you saying 'You are not a painter', then by all means paint and that voice will be shattered."
> ~ Vincent Van Gogh

Luckily, there is a key to getting out of the trap. You simply have to understand that the only thing wrong with you is that you think there is something wrong with you. Or to put it another way – God doesn't make anything less than perfection. Your weaknesses and vulnerabilities are an essential part of you. They are as critical to the miracle of who you are as your strengths.

The "Half a Loaf" Syndrome

Comparing ourselves with others to see if we measure up is a very familiar past time for most of us. We do it with family, friends, neighbors, coworkers and even people we don't know. And most of the time it leaves us feeling like we are missing something – like we don't quite measure up somehow. For example, have you ever found yourself comparing your life to the life of someone rich and famous and thinking "If only I had their life?" What were you thinking about them or their lives that was so enticing? Was it the money? Maybe it was the luxury items they have or their ability to travel to exotic places. Maybe it was the respect they command or their ability to rub shoulders with interesting and powerful people.

If I had to guess, you rarely if ever, gave any thought to the downside of what it must be like being that person you were comparing yourself to. What price did they have to pay to get where they are, or to maintain it? What hidden adversities or weaknesses do they have to struggle with day-to-day as a human being? What things are going on behind the public curtain that make up the unseen aspects of how it feels to be them? And if you knew the cost – the price of being that person – would you still wish for their life?

When we compare ourselves to others we usually do it from the "half-a-loaf" perspective. That is, we look at the good half and base all our comparisons on that part – finding ourselves lacking in the comparison. We fail to even consider the other half of the loaf – the costs, worries and issues that come as an inextricable part of the good half. You have surely heard that there is no "free lunch." Well there is also no success without cost. No one gets all the good stuff in life for free. The question is whether the results are worth the price you must pay for them.

> "To dream of the person you want to be is a waste of the person you are. Take what you have right now and cherish it!"
>
> ~ Anonymous

Telling you to just "stop comparing yourself with others" is only mildly helpful. Yes, the more you can refrain from unfair comparisons with others the better. But if you are anything like me, you'll never manage to avoid it completely. So instead, remember the half-a-loaf syndrome when you are doing the comparison. Yes, that other person might have something or be something you wish you had or were. But ask yourself at what price it was achieved. If you don't have any way of knowing then guess at some likely scenarios. When you have considered the "whole loaf" for a while then ask yourself – "Would I be willing to pay that price to have it?" If you still answer yes, then you must face the hardest question of all – what are you going to do about it?

It's All Part of the Puzzle

Alright, so maybe those comparisons with others are unfair but what about the real flaws you have? You know those things you are missing or can't seem to get right? Not to worry. Even those things have their rightful place in an *Exactly Right Life*. Think of it this way. You are a puzzle piece. Your strengths and talents are like the round bits that stick out on a puzzle piece. Your flaws are like the cutout parts of the pieces. Like a puzzle, you need both parts in order to fit together with other people and to fill your unique place in the world.

Your cut-out flaws make room for others to connect to you. Your stand-out strengths allow you to make a difference in other's lives. Without both sides of you, there would be little hope of finding the connections that allow us to come together and create a life that is greater than any one of us can experience alone.

We simply think about it backwards – we think that our flaws are what separate us from other people. They're not. It's our desperate attempts to cover up, ignore or completely eliminate our flaws that keep people away. You can't hide one side of you without also hiding some parts of the other side. When you work so hard to mask your flaws, some of your greatness gets covered up in the process.

I don't suggest you just give in to parts of yourself that you don't like and just "be ok" with them. If they truly don't work for you then by all means give them some attention and try to improve upon them. It's just at some point they are as "fixed" as they are going to get and nothing more can be gained by concentrating on the flaws. Instead, let them be and seek out those miraculous connections that are only possible when you let all of you shine through.

Exercise 15:
Puzzle Pieces

O.k., it is time to strip down and get naked – metaphorically at least! It's time to talk about the real you – chubby butt-cheeks and all. Don't worry, you're alone with the mirror; nobody is watching. The idea here is to sit with yourself and let your flaws come to the surface, so that you can make peace with them. Be compassionate and truthful with yourself – put it all out there as you do this exercise.

As we mentioned, each one of us has weaknesses and strengths that make us like a puzzle piece. Our strengths are the gifts we give to ourselves, God, and those around us. Our weaknesses are the areas where others can support and give to us. Just like a puzzle piece, we need to contribute and be contributed to in order to fit into the whole picture.

1. List what you see as your flaws here. List the flaws that annoy you the most first:

2. There are two main things to notice about weaknesses. One is that our flaws have a lesson to teach. If you were to embrace each flaw mentioned, one by one, and say to it: "I trust you are here to teach me", what might be the lesson? List the lesson you think each one of your flaws is trying to teach you. A few examples are listed below.

Example lessons one might learn from flaws:

✦ The lesson is that I need others who have strengths in this area. I will ask for help.

✦ Change "ain't gonna happen". It is what it is. The lesson is acceptance. There is nothing wrong with me.

✦ I want to improve and grow regarding this. It will help me with relationships, health, etc. The lesson is that I have it within me to make changes and realize my desires.

✦ I've let others' opinions influence me but the truth is, I really don't care about this. I'm letting it go.

3. The second main thing to notice about each "flaw" is that it isn't necessarily negative. Remember, other people need a chance to shine too! If you do what you are good at, and they do what they are good at, we all get to create something together. In the area below, list how some of your flaws have allowed others to connect with you, and/or share their strengths.

Breaking Free Of Addiction To External Approval

It's important to understand that *Exactly Right* is more than just "fixing what's wrong" or changing your actions and habits. It requires a fundamental shift in how you relate to yourself and your life. For most of us, it's our default relationship to ourselves – how you think about you – that is at the heart of the problem.

Most of us don't begin with an independent idea of who we are. If we did, we might not feel the need to "find ourselves" at some point in life. The good news is you aren't lost. You simply cannot separate what you think of you from what others think of you. Or as a friend more appropriately put it: "It's not what I think of me, or even what you think of me, but what I think you think of me that's the problem!"

> "We often fear being rejected so much that we reject ourselves first before anyone else has the chance."
> ~ Anonymous

Often, our idea about who we are is completely entangled in a never-ending cycle of approval seeking. Do you like me now? Am I ok? Did I get it right? It's like walking through life mentally repeating that movie line "We're not worthy!" – like some sort of mantra to explain how we feel about ourselves. We are constantly looking to others to validate that we are good enough. Unfortunately, external validation is never enough… As long as your self worth is based upon external approval, you will always have to "check-in" to make sure that you are okay. And your experience of yourself will change at the whim of the "approval meter."

It's often the fear of being separate that has us seek that external validation. We want very much to be a part of something – to feel like we are on the inside. And we believe others have to approve of us and let us in or we will be alone. Ultimately, that fear of separation comes from an inability or unwillingness to trust yourself and God.

If you want to find who you really are and what works for you, you are going to have to break the chains of dependence on outside approval. You must separate out who you are from what others think, and finally know and trust in what God has made. You have been created with all the tools you need to live a life that fulfills you. One in which you get to do and be exactly the way you were designed. This doesn't mean that you don't take advice and consider others' input. It just means that you trust that your own way, guided by your heart and by God, is good enough to lead you to your *Exactly Right Life*.

Get More Free Stuff

More is available!

Additional tools, articles, and recorded meditations have

been created to support your journey.

Check it out at:

www.MoveMountainsInitiative.com

on the Get More tab

For this chapter, look for:

5.1 Letting Go Meditation
5.2 The Jericho Exercise

My Thoughts

_____

_____

_____

_____

_____

_____

_____

_____

_____

_____

_____

_____

_____

_____

_____

_____

_____

Colors of the Soul

"Emotions are the colors of the soul; they are spectacular and incredible. When you don't feel, the world becomes dull and colorless."

~Wm. Paul Young

*Getting connected
means applying whatever practice allows you to
move out of your head and into your heart.
Your heart space is where the Design of You
lives. It is also the conduit through which Spirit
can communicate with you.*

~ Exactly Right Philosophy

6

Focus on
What Really Matters

ocus is the lynchpin to living a life you love. It is the word I use to describe the practice of getting in touch with your higher self and communing directly with God.

You were designed to work best in a particular one-of-a-kind way.

Certain things bring you joy and happiness. Certain ways of living bring out the very best in you, allowing your presence to be a blessing to others. Unfortunately, most of us are not consciously aware of what those ways are. Most people search their entire life for the right way to live.

The good news is...

that you were also designed to inherently recognize those things that best fit with the *Design of You*. This recognition is often blocked from your view by all the busyness of life and the disempowering stories you hold on to.

Hopefully what you learned and experienced in the last three chapters about:

◆ Taking a step back,

◆ Becoming more conscious of your stories, and

◆ Letting go of your extra baggage

has allowed you to create new stories from the heart that better serve you. Little by little, your effort at loving self-reflection will help you break through the illusions you hold about yourself and your life. It can also train you to connect more fully to your heart and to God. It's through this sacred connection you can see more clearly the way that you were made to live.

✦ Practice Listening To Spirit ✦

Focus is not just about concentrating on what we want to the exclusion of everything else. It is also learning to understand all of the feedback we are getting from Spirit.

We ask Spirit for what we desire or for information on the best way to live; but what must accompany the request is a willingness to hear the answer we receive. Even if (maybe especially if) it is not the answer we were looking for.

To a large degree this chapter is about practice. Achieving mastery of Focus (connecting, communing, awakening and realizing how to live our best life) requires a lifetime of practice, application and refinement.

So get started now, right where you are. Each little refinement brings you one step closer to your *Exactly Right Life*.

This chapter is about working on your own sacred connection. It's about discovering what allows you to tune into Spirit, listen to your own heart, and start living the life you were made for. You will become more comfortable seeking guidance, wisdom, and support from higher sources. You will remember to ask for help outside yourself when you need it. You'll also learn how to recognize and appreciate your own beauty, strength and courage.

Connecting to your heart

I have found that tuning into your own inner wisdom and to that sacred connection to Spirit, is essential to understanding how to live a fulfilling and satisfying life. I've also discovered that it doesn't take hours on a meditation cushion to get tuned in. Sometimes it takes as little as seeing something beautiful or reading something inspiring to make the connection. The key is finding things that allow you to feel that you have access to your own heart and to the wisdom that comes from beyond your thinking mind.

To most effectively work through the exercises in this chapter, I encourage you to set aside a block of time just for you. Choose a quiet, comfortable space. Then take the time to get centered and free from any mental distractions before diving in. This not only assists you with a clearer mental state from which to work through the exercises, it also helps to open up your heart so that the answers you discover provide useful insights into those most important aspects of how you want to live.

Exercise 16:
What Does Connection Mean To You?

Connecting to your heart and Spirit can happen anywhere at any time. It can be as simple as taking a moment in nature to smell a flower, watch a beautiful sunset, or listen to the birds sing. It can be admiring a work of art, appreciating a '57 Corvette, or listening to a song that lifts your spirit, and makes you want to sing along with childlike glee. Where there is light, God is. It is that simple. When your heart sings, when you feel joyful for whatever reason, you are connected. You know because you can feel it. Your heart is open and tuned in.

So what does it take for you to get connected? What things, practices, or situations enable you to get calm and centered so that you can listen to your heart and to Spirit? For some of you this is a foreign concept, or you may have to look hard to remember if you have ever felt connected. Don't worry; trust that you have the ability to recognize it when it happens. For others, this connection is a long time friend. In this exercise you simply want to explore or deepen what it is like for you to connect.

1. Describe what being connected feels like for you, or what you imagine it would feel like.

2. Identify those situations, places, circumstances, practices and/or physical objects that most easily bring you that feeling of connection you described above. (You may want to refer back to Exercise 8 in Chapter 3: Identify and Create Your Own Personal Retreat.) List them below.

3. Now that you've thought about what connection looks like for you, take some time and actually connect. Stop what you are doing, take at least ten minutes and go connect. Go Ahead… connect… then come back to the workbook.

Make a commitment to yourself...

to connect regularly. It can be simple (like noticing the beauty of a flower) or more involved (like meditation). If you need more ideas, feel free to use the resources from other chapters or from www. MoveMountainsInitiative.com. Just get started. The more you practice, the more natural it becomes. And you'll soon notice that life is looking better all the time.

Seeking guidance and wisdom

The value of connecting is that it allows you to get input on some of the great questions of life. Questions like – "Who am I?" "Why am I here?" and "How can I be happy?" You probably won't get the whole answer all at once – no matter how connected you are. So take it slow and give it time. Also remember that there is no question too small, unimportant or inappropriate to ask. So take your questions into your connection time and listen – you may just get the information you need to steer you in the right direction.

Exercise 17:
What Would You Like To Ask?

In looking for answers it is very helpful to know the questions! So what questions do you want answered? What's weighing on your heart? If you had access to your highest, best self – if you were plugged directly into the presence of God and could ask anything – what would you ask? Take some time to really think about this. Then list some questions or issues below:

_____

_____

_____

_____

_____

_____

_____

Once you have some questions or issues you would like to take to Spirit, I recommend the following practice:

1. Get connected using whatever method works for you. A regular time and place is useful but not required. It is also likely to require more than one sitting, so consider setting aside times for regular ongoing practice.

2. Take one of the questions or issues you listed above and focus on it as you connect. (You can take a couple of related ones into your session but too many can just muddy the waters and reduce the clarity of the guidance you can expect.)

3. Then ask the question aloud to yourself and Spirit.

4. Listen and feel the response you get. Don't judge what you feel, see or hear – or what you don't feel, see, or hear. Oftentimes the answer doesn't come until later. Sometimes the answers you do get are unclear, particularly if you are just starting out and don't have a lot of practice. Sometimes the answer is blocked by high emotion or attachment to a particular answer or specific result. That's normal. Give it time – there is nothing wrong with you or the way you are doing it! Simply become aware of your experience. (You may want to keep a record of your experiences in your journal. See Get More 3.3)

5. If you do get some useful feedback it is important to act on it. That way you can "road test" it, and see how best to respond so it really works for you. Remember, however, that this testing phase is not done in a vacuum. You are checking for workability and how to apply the information you are getting, but you are still walking with God and staying aware of further guidance when it comes.

6. Keep track of and record the results of number five. This allows you to see your growth over time. It also allows you to see patterns emerge in your conversations with God.

7. Rinse and repeat.

✦ *Practice Together* ✦

Consider participating in some group connection. Just as meditation is often more powerful in a group, so too, connection can be extraordinary in collaboration with others. All of the participants can connect and then ask questions and have answers come out of co-creation. This can be a very powerful tool to get and keep direction in the lives of the group members.

Realizing Your Desires

"Ask and you shall receive" is a universal truth. This often doesn't feel true, however, and is where most of us falter. We falter because sometimes the best answer for us is NO, but we just don't want to hear it. Perhaps we are only looking for the answer we want or expect. Sometimes, we have moved on to another issue entirely by the time we get the answer to our previous concern. We may have even forgotten what we asked for in the first place. Any of these situations can make it seem like we're getting no answers — when really we are simply failing to notice the responses that are coming our way.

I have learned through much trial and error that there is a discipline to receiving. It looks something like the following:

✦ Trust – God never fails to come through if what you asked is for your well-being;

✦ Expect – That the universe will provide; you are worthy to receive;

✦ Let go – Of how it should look; it may very well not look like you expect but it will be for your greatest good;

✦ Stay aware – And notice any inklings or gut feelings, serendipity, synchronicities, repetitive messages, dreams, promptings, visions, resources, feedback from other people, or that special "ah-ha" feeling of just knowing;

✦ Act – According to what you receive;

✦ Express gratefulness – For the response to your requests or desires.

Pay particular attention to steps 5 & 6 in the previous exercise of "What Would You Like to Ask?" Unless you have been connecting in this way for a while you may have a very "fuzzy" connection at first – like a radio station out of tune. Furthermore, you may judge, discount, add to, or misinterpret the information you get. That is why it is important to test it – do something with it – and observe the results. Ask yourself, "What happened when I followed the guidance I received? How did it feel? What effect did it have?" Then you want to connect and check in to get more information. It is about adjusting your aim more than making the perfect shot the first time.

Give Spirit time and space to work. Keep taking action, making notes and adjusting as you go. You will be amazed at what shows up! Don't give up or discredit your efforts just because you don't receive any immediate answers. As evidenced by the examples given above, guidance can manifest in many ways and often not during your connection session. It is also important not to get hung up on getting the right answer. Often we ask for things and expect a certain response. This limits our relationship with Spirit. Remember, if we want things to be better than we could have imagined, we must be open to things we weren't already aware of. We must be willing to ask; be alert and receptive to the answers; and then be willing to do the work to fulfill on God's guidance. Trust in the Universe to do its part while you do yours.

Starting With The Heart

God has a path just for you to follow. Your job is to learn the path that was designed for you and then walk it. You do this by accepting God's overwhelmingly generous invitation to walk with you, in collaboration for your greatest life – the life you were made to live.

~Exactly Right Philosophy

Why do I keep encouraging you to "listen to your heart?" It's because that's where true self-knowledge begins. Why do I keep encouraging you to connect? Because connecting allows you to access information that's normally hidden from your view. It helps you turn down the mental noise so you can get in tune with yourself and with things bigger than yourself.

Your connection journey starts with your heart because that's where the closest thing to a blueprint of you resides. You desire certain things for a reason, you feel passionately about certain things for a reason. Your heart cries out and asks questions unique to you because your heart – like you – is one of a kind. It makes sense, then, to get in touch with those needs and wants that are unique to you. Your heart is the guide that gives you insight into the *Design of You*. And it's that unique design that forms the foundation of your own *Exactly Right Life*. So if you want to Focus, start with your heart.

Get More Free Stuff

More is available!

Additional tools, articles, and recorded meditations have

been created to support your journey.

Check it out at:

www.MoveMountainsInitiative.com

on the Get More tab

For this chapter, look for:

6.1 Hearing Back From Spirit
6.2 Answer And Idea Bank
6.3 Spiritual Guidance Tools

My Thoughts

_____

_____

_____

_____

_____

_____

_____

_____

_____

_____

_____

_____

_____

_____

_____

_____

_____

_____

_____

Love the Becoming

"You'll always be in the process of 'becoming'. Love the 'becoming' and you'll love life."

~ Matthew Ferry

The special Design of You is written on your heart, engraved by Spirit. Following what's written on your heart, and living out your unique story, provides a critical addition to the tapestry of life as a whole. Humanity is enriched and all of our lives become greater for it.

~ Exactly Right Philosophy

Choose A Fulfilling Path

How do you combine all of the work you've done so far, and all that you have discovered, into some kind of coherent whole that helps you live a more fulfilling life? This chapter is designed to help answer that question. As you work through the material that follows, continue to question any judgments or assumptions about who you can be and what you can have. While society and other people have opinions about what you should do, only you can choose a way of living that is *Exactly Right* for you. As Oprah Winfrey so eloquently put it, "Understand that the right to choose your own path is a sacred privilege. Use it. Dwell in possibility."

We each have our own individual way to most effectively live a fulfilling life. Our job is to align our actions with that "way." Doing so can manifest itself on an everyday basis as satisfaction, fulfillment, joy, ease, vitality, and just plain old happiness. It requires that you bring the best of you to the forefront. That includes your talents, passions, and gifts, along with your vision for how you want to experience your life.

Illuminating ✦Purpose✦

"Purpose is the hope-filled glow of a meaningful life. It illuminates all circumstances of living."
~ Cecile Burzynski

As we look more deeply in those areas, it will be useful to revisit some of your responses from earlier chapters. You many want to jot down a few notes, or simply review your responses to the following questions in preparation for moving on to the next exercise:

◆ Exercise 5, Question #2 – Three to six words that are most empowering to you when you think of your *Exactly Right Life*

◆ Exercise 6 – Dream Board

◆ Exercise 9, Step #2, Question #6 – Labels you're the proudest of

◆ Exercise 12 – Design of a new story from your heart

◆ *Three Great Questions* ◆

Your unique path will naturally include your passions, your dreams, your talents and what makes sense. It is not a recipe for perfection. It is a design for workability. It is the place where all the different aspects of yourself align – where the whole is greater than the sum of the parts.

> *[This] is not a goal to be the best, a strategy to be the best, a*
> *plan to be the best. It is an understanding of what you can be*
> *the best at. The distinction is absolutely crucial. ~Jim Collins*

The concept involves developing a deep understanding of three key dimensions, as identified in the three circles on the following page. Defining your own path is about developing a life that's as close to the intersection of these three circles as possible. These questions are modified versions of those discovered by Jim Collins in his book Good to Great[1].

---

1   Jim Collins, Good to Great: Why Some Companies Make the Leap... and Others Don't (New York: Harper Collins 2001).

Exercise 18:
Defining Your Unique Path

To get the most out of this exercise, detach yourself from what you're currently doing in your life. Rise above any doubts, fears, or other obstacles. Don't judge your dreams. Know that you are capable of doing what is in your heart. Step back, quiet your mind by applying the Heart Level Reflection or another connection method of your choosing. When you feel connected and ready to create from the heart, consider the questions in the diagram below. To help you better understand the questions and begin to answer them for yourself, I have broken them down in more detail on the following pages. Take as much time as you need to fully explore the questions before writing out your answers.

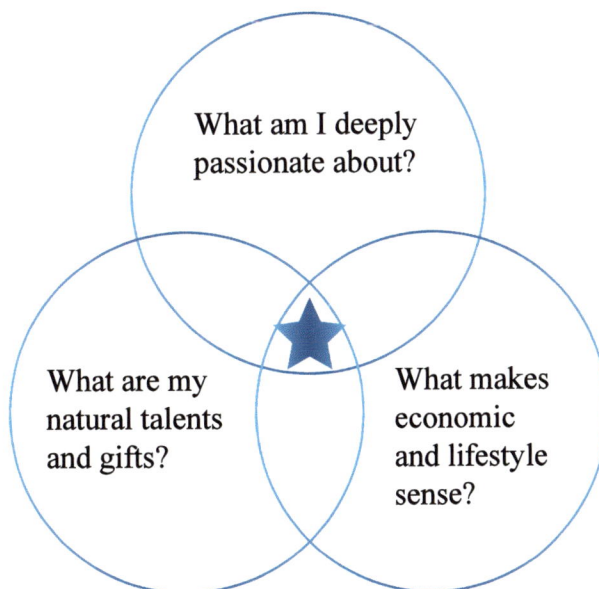

What am I deeply passionate about?

What are my natural talents and gifts?

What makes economic and lifestyle sense?

1. What am I deeply passionate about?

What situations ignite my passions?

What am I deeply passionate about?

What settings bring out the best in me?

What fascinates me?

What is my heart telling me to do?

2. What are my natural gifts and talents?

What do I do best?

What are my natural talents and gifts?

What do people compliment me on, or come to me for?

What comes easily to me? What am I successful at?

What work or activity is deeply satisfying to me?

What is the perfect lifestyle for me? How do I want to live?

3. *What makes economic and lifestyle sense?*

What makes economic and lifestyle sense?

How close am I to living this way already?

How can I make a viable living doing what I love?

What is the least I can afford to make if I'm doing what I love? What do I want to make or earn?

Where It All Comes Together

You'll likely need multiple visioning sessions over a period of time while the ideas simmer. Keep documenting your thoughts, dreams, and ideas as they come to you. You may also want to brainstorm with people you know and trust. Take a look at the Get Mores listed at the end of this chapter to further assist you. The full text of these and other Get Mores are available at www.MoveMountainsInitiative.com.

When you get reasonably clear about the questions above, find that quiet, inspiring place to imagine and dream (with no interruptions). Invite Spirit into your session to guide you as you envision the place where the answers to these questions come together. Give yourself time to let the ideas flow. Then write down the essence of the answer you see and the good things that come to mind as you think about it. Have faith that the answers you find will converge into clear and inspiring guidance. Know that you can love what you're doing, be great at it, and have your life work.

> "Whatever is important to you, whatever brings meaning to your life – may this be your special path."
> ~ Susan Squellati Florence

4. My Unique Path

In the space below write down your ideas about how the Three Great Questions come together for you. Essentially, this convergence provides a snapshot of how you tick – a window into the *Design of You*. While there may be more to learn and understand, it is a great starting point for discovering your own path to follow.

My Unique Path

Exercise 19:
Aligning Your Life To Your Unique Path

Fulfillment—a life well lived—is about creating a life that really works for you, based upon your personal truth and staying aligned to that truth. As Dolly Parton wisely proclaimed, "Find out who you are and do it on purpose!" So in this exercise, look at the life you're currently living and its various dimensions. Now that you've begun to consider the components needed for your own *Exactly Right Life*, take a moment to see how close you already are to living that life. You might be closer than you think!

5. Listed on the next page are key Life Dimensions. Take a look at them with your life in mind. Feel free to add or delete any based on what's important to you. Now take what you defined for your Unique Path and assess whether it is already aligned with your path, or not.

Life Dimensions	Aligned	Not Aligned
Home		
Work		
Family		
Friends		
Social Life		
Fun		
Personal Growth		
Health		
Creativity		
Spiritual/Religious Pursuits		
Fitness		

6. What are the top 2-3 areas that you want to shift to make your life align more with your *Exactly Right Life*? Think big!

Making successful shifts in any one of our life dimensions generally requires changes in our thoughts, supporting habits, the actions we take, and the amount of time and energy we are willing to devote to that dimension. For most of us, when we admit the truth to ourselves, we have a pretty good idea of what we need to focus on, modify and improve. But many of us struggle with how to put that "knowing" into practice. We want to do it right but often get stuck in figuring out the best way to get started. Here's a helpful hint... Just start, you can refine the methods along the way.

Of course before we can take the first steps, we must truly buy-in to the plan to act. Our hearts must be in it as much as our minds or we will falter when issues arise. Consider the following steps to help you get started:

◆ Understand why these certain areas have not been working for you, so that you can wisely create habits or changes that will work.

◆ Visualize yourself thinking/acting/being the shift you want to make. Keep visualizing until you can truly feel it and it feels yummy and right.

◆ If the specific course of action is still not clear, consider experimenting with some new approaches first or doing some additional research. You might even want to brainstorm with a friend or mentor.

◆ Admit the truth about how much time and energy you are willing to spend to make changes in this area. If you aren't willing to invest more time and energy here then pick a different area.

7. Given the areas you have identified that you would like to shift, pick one or two of them and then list two specific changes in your thoughts, habits or actions that you believe could make a difference. Note: If you have more than two dimensions or you see more than two actions to take feel free to make a list of all that you see. I recommend, however, that you work on one or two dimensions or changes to a particular dimension at a time. Give those changes time to work and then come back and add in more. Avoid the temptation to bite off too much at one time.

Exercise 20:
Creating Your *Exactly Right* Story

Okay, it's time! It's time to let your dreams flow, and let your imagination run for a little while. Take a few moments now and write a story about a life that makes your heart sing. What is the *Exactly Right Life* for you? What are you doing? Where are you? What is around you? Who is there with you? How are you feeling about your life? Incorporate the essence of that magical place where your three circles intersect, along with the shifts you know you need to make as if you've already made them. Remember, you are looking for things you can actually start doing right where you are with the resources you already have.

Don't worry about telling the perfect story now. You can come back and change this anytime you want. Just play. Invent. It may be farfetched and wild, or it may be common place. The only thing that matters is that it makes you happy and excited to think about it. Tell the story:

Once you have your story written, take a look at it and see how many of the appealing aspects of it are already in your life. Look at one or two that may be missing, but are easy to get started on, and resolve to do something about them in the next couple of weeks. It's also important to start talking about the changes you want to make. Start including others in what you are up to so that you can begin building the support you need to achieve your goals.

Get More Free Stuff

More is available!

Additional tools, articles, and recorded meditations have

been created to support your journey.

Check it out at:

www.MoveMountainsInitiative.com

on the Get More tab

For this chapter, look for:

7.1 How Do You Know What Really Inspires You

7.2 Others Can See Your Talent (Interviews)

7.3 How To Know If It's Time To Get A Coach

7.4 Life Dimensions: Examples of Empowering Habits

My Thoughts

_____

_____

_____

_____

_____

_____

_____

_____

_____

_____

_____

_____

_____

_____

_____

_____

_____

Being Great

"Not everyone can be famous, but everybody can be great… because greatness is determined by service."

~Dr. Martin Luther King, Jr.

"Other people may be there to help us,
teach us, guide us along our path,
but the lesson to be learned is always ours."

~ Author Unknown

Connect With Others

Our connections and relationships largely determine our experience of life. The three major connections are connection to self, God and others. Now that you have looked at your connection to yourself in the Erase phase and to Spirit in the Focus phase, it is time to look at your relationship with others, so that you can effectively create your *Exactly Right Life*.

Life happens out in the world – in our interaction with others. It is almost impossible to achieve any great success alone. Why should it be surprising then, that we need others on our team in order to live our *Exactly Right Life*? As you begin to refine your own unique path in life, you will discover that it helps to find people who understand you and are excited by what you're doing. It's also helpful to get feedback from those people whose perspective you value. As you test it for yourself and interact with others you will get some valuable information. Keep asking questions: What works? What doesn't? How does it make me feel? How does it affect others? Who genuinely supports me?

Crossing
✦ Paths ✦

"No love, no friendship, can cross the path of our destiny without leaving some mark on it forever."
~Francois Mocuriac

Exercise 21:
Talk About Your Dreams, Early & Often

This is where you start sharing your *Exactly Right* story, and the actions you are taking, with others who can support you. If you don't know how to get started or if it seems a bit scary, start with those you trust the most. This will also allow your loved ones to support you and give you feedback and encouragement as you start making changes.

Name three key people from different areas of your life who you want to share with – people who have a perspective you value and will give you honest feedback. Be clear about how you would like them to support you, as it may be different for each person.

Name	Their Gift or Perspective	Desired Support

Now schedule some time in your calendar in the next couple of weeks to share with each of these people. Sometimes, sharing your *Exactly Right* story with others adds energy, insight, and momentum to bring it to life. It may also inspire others to create their own *Exactly Right* story. Ask them for their suggestions and invite them to support you.

Exercise 22:
Who Are My People?

Choose Thoughtfully

When you are redesigning and making positive changes in your life, you may find that some people are not supportive of your new, more authentic way of living. In some cases they are actively opposed to it. Whether you have been conscious of it or not, you have surrounded yourself with people who support your habitual way of living and thinking. Some of them may be unwilling or unable to change with you.

I recommend that you avoid forcing yourself to change back and forth to satisfy all the people in your life. Also avoid forcing others to change for you. You can invite them to come with you, but you cannot make them. Instead, focus on creating connections and relationships that support you. Remember, everyone has their own path to follow.

Take a look back at Chapter 7 and review your own *Exactly Right* story. This is the story you wrote that describes what your fulfilling life would look like. You may have heard the phrase "life is a team sport". Creating your own *Exactly Right Life* is going to take input, help, and interaction with others. Now consider:

1. How do you want others to support you?

2. What type of people do you gravitate towards? It is helpful to think about the people you know, or would like to get to know better. Who stands out to you? What about them stands out?

3. Are there any people in your life that are NOT a fit for you? What are the characteristics that make them incompatible?

4. Given the above, begin naming your personal *Exactly Right* team.

Sometimes you think people will be interested in your dreams and they won't be. Some of the people that are interested will surprise you. Don't take their agreement or disagreement personally. Continue looking for the people who are a good fit for your new way of living.

Exercise 23:
Crab Fishing

The Crab Syndrome

Often, when we change the way we have been living, we run head-long into the "crab syndrome." The name of the syndrome comes from the behavior of live crabs. You'll find that a bucket of crabs is often left uncovered. This is not from oversight, it's because there is no worry that they will escape. Whenever one of the crabs begins to make it over the side of the bucket to freedom, the other crabs in the bucket will reach up with their claws, grab hold of the escaping crab and pull it back down.

Some of the people in our lives are like that. When we begin to grow and change they will try and keep us where we are – whether through nay-saying, or through actions to block or even sabotage our efforts. It's crucial to form connections that will support us to counteract the crab syndrome. There is a natural tendency to fall back into familiar, old patterns. The crabs in our lives make it almost impossible not to. Part of building support includes identifying and cleaning out the crabs that stand in our way.

As you may have guessed from the title of this exercise, it's time to identify the people who represent roadblocks to your *Exactly Right Life*. It is important to remember that I am not asking you to cut these people from your life. Many people seem like crabs because you have trained them to react according to your old habits and behavior. It's your job to share with them your new way of living. You may become an inspiration to them and they just might become one of your biggest supporters. If not, it's okay. Of course if you identify abusive, unhealthy or unworkable relationships, this is also the chance to end them.

1. What behaviors in others bring you down, slow your progress, and keep you stuck?

2. Who in your life falls into these categories?

3. How have you trained them to be crabs? (For example: when people give John honest feedback that he doesn't like, he gets mad at them and quits talking. Then they stop giving him the feedback he needs.)

It's important, as you evaluate your relationships, to not only look at the other people and how they behave toward you – but also look at what part you play in that relationship. How have you contributed to the way the relationship is going? Also tell the truth about how much effort you are willing to put forth to maintain and/or grow that particular relationship. In this process you may find that there are some people you will need to let go of. You may find that you have a lot of work to do to "retrain" some of the people you care about to support your new ways of living. Regardless of what you find, I recommend that you take it slow and don't make rash decisions. Good relationships are precious things. Approach all of them with compassion and understanding, but also with a healthy dose of truth, so that you can find where they fit in your *Exactly Right Life*.

Exercise 24:
Watch Out For Speed Bumps

Speed Bumps

So why don't most of us naturally go out and build support to help us live our dreams? Why don't we share our deepest desires with others? Mostly it seems like a dangerous or scary proposition. We think that we'll look silly or that people will think we're nuts if we share ourselves that deeply. We want to fit in so we fear rocking the boat in our relationships, and in the world. We may fear that if we share, someone's going to steal our "great ideas." They are going to go make a success of our dreams and leave us holding the bag.

Many of us also get wrapped up in the need to be unique and different. If we share an idea, and someone else is also doing it, then we think "Oh well, that's worthless now", and we give up. We behave as if our idea or dream only has merit if we are the only one in the whole world doing it. However, no great idea has ever made an impact in the world without the involvement of others. Gandhi was not the only one to come up with the idea of non-violent resistance, and it would have made little difference anyway without the thousands of people who were willing to actually stand up with him.

Sharing what you are learning and creating with other people can be a bit unnerving, but it can also be amazingly useful. When you talk about it with others, it can seem more real for you. As you explain it you refine your own ideas and get feedback. You may also find encouragement to keep going when you get stuck. Perhaps one of the most useful benefits of sharing is that it takes away your ability to hide. People start watching you to see what you are creating and to see if you are doing the work you said you were going to do. While this may feel like a lot of pressure, it may just be the thing you need to keep taking positive action.

1. What stops you from sharing yourself with others?

2. What parts of yourself or your dreams are you most afraid of letting others know about?

3. What's the worst thing that could happen if you were to share your dreams? How likely is it that something terrible would happen? (When you look at this, you may notice that it isn't really scary enough to keep you from sharing.)

4. What's the best thing that could happen if you share your dreams?

5. Name a few people you would love to share your dreams with.

Consider this: you will never know if someone will support you unless you give them a chance. The bonus exercise is to schedule a specific time in your calendar to meet and talk with each of these people and share your dreams with them. When you do, your only task is to authentically share with them and get honest feedback. Don't expect them to react in a particular way. Let it be okay if they love it, if they hate it, or even if they don't understand.

6. When you are done, write down what you learned from the interaction.

Playing Well With Others

Other people can be the source of some of our greatest pleasures and of our most painful hurts. They can be "the wind beneath our wings" or the "thorn in our sides." But either way, there is no getting away from the fact that we live in a world with other people. So what can you do to stack the deck in your favor? To set it up so that others become a consistent source of support and inspiration?

A great place to start is to use your heart as a "people meter" to help you sort and navigate amongst those with whom you will come in contact as you go about your life. The good news is that there are more "great people" available to any of us than we could possibly develop and maintain relationships with. The problem is not finding them... The problem is sorting through so many choices to identify those people you want to add into your life.

We have a certain amount of people that are part of our lives by default at one time or another. Family, coworkers and neighbors, for example, are folks we rarely get to pick. As you go about developing your *Exactly Right Life* you will naturally interact with these people and determine which of them still fit, and which you will maintain a less involved relationship with.

> "[I] keep on trying to find a way of becoming what I would so like to be, and could be, if there weren't any other people living in the world."
> ~ Anne Frank

In addition to those people you are involved with by default, however, I recommend actively cultivating and adding people from beyond those circles so that you can grow your team of what I like to call your Power People. Who are they and how do you identify them? They may or may not be the smartest, wealthiest, most successful, or most powerful folks you know. Your Power People are the ones that have you remember who you truly are. They make you feel powerful as you live life according to your dreams and unique design. To help you identify those people, look for some of the following qualities:

◆ Who does your heart cry out to be around? You may not be able to explain it, but you just feel happy and empowered when you are with them.

◆ Who inspires and uplifts you? Who seems to light up the room and lift your spirits no matter what mood you are in?

◆ Who makes you live up to your own promises? Sometimes we get more out of the one who kicks our butt, than the one who pats us on the shoulder. Who refuses to let you settle for less than you are capable of? Who doesn't let you give up on living your dreams?

◆ Who sees you for who you really are? They don't care about what you wear, the car you drive or whether you're having a bad hair day... They only want to deal with the real you. And when you forget who that is, they are quick to remind you.

◆ Who inspires you to do more? Just being around them makes you ask the tough question, "Am I doing all that I can do to have what I say I want?"

◆ Who reminds you not to take yourself or your life so seriously? They bring out the fun and playful side of you. They call to the childlike wonder of your soul.

◆ Who makes you remember your heart and your connection to God? When you are around them you feel connected or you are reminded to reconnect.

Consider these qualities as you develop your relationships. Consider also, which one (or more) of these qualities you provide for others? You will find that the most powerful relationships are often those in which both parties are Power People for each other.

As you grow your circle of support, remember that this is not a race or a contest. You don't get more points for going faster or slower. You don't get a prize for having the most people or getting by with the fewest. The whole purpose is to find the right mix of people who fit with who you are, and who help you (and everyone around you) to experience their own *Exactly Right Life*.

Get More Free Stuff

More is available!

Additional tools, articles, and recorded meditations have

been created to support your journey.

Check it out at:

www.MoveMountainsInitiative.com

on the Get More tab

For this chapter, look for:

8.1 Sharing the New You
8.2 Take the New You Out for a Test Drive

My Thoughts

_____

_____

_____

_____

_____

_____

_____

_____

_____

_____

_____

_____

_____

_____

_____

Reveling The Real You

"The people and circumstances around me do not make me what I am, they reveal who I am."

~ Dr. Laura Schlessinger

"Dreams pass into the reality of action.
From the actions stems the dream again;
and this interdependence produces
the highest form of living."

~Anaïs Nin

9

Get Into Balanced Action

Balanced Action is an old concept that has some practical applications in our modern lives. And while I don't claim to be a master of this process by any means, I do love the practice.

The basic idea is to get connected, calm, and centered so that you know when to act, and how to act, in any given moment. Often the timing of an action is as important as the action itself. Balanced Action has the feeling of being "in the zone" – you don't have to think, you already know what to do. It is an amazing state of being filled with peace, confidence, and connectedness. And you know when you are in it. It comes from aligning the actions you want to take with the guidance you receive from Spirit. It shows up as a feeling of "rightness" when these things align.

Happiness of
✦ Harmony ✦

"Happiness is when what you think, what you say, and what you do are in harmony."
~Mahatma Gandhi

Exercise 25:
What Is Balanced Action?

Seven key areas of Balanced Action are listed below. Assess yourself in each area. Where are you now? Where do you realistically want to be? This is a great way to see which area deserves the most attention, or where it would be the most fun (or inspiring) to raise your score.

Put a check mark where you are now and a star where you want to be.

1. *Finding The Zone*

One of the biggest blocks to Balanced Action is that when we are not in the zone, taking the time to get there doesn't seem convenient or interesting. It's important, however, to develop the habit of stopping every time you notice you are out of the zone, because time spent out of the zone can be very costly. When we are operating in a distracted or frustrated state of mind, we just don't perform at our best. We may even undo some of the good work we've already accomplished.

How Are You Doing?
How often do you feel "in the zone" in your life? Where do you want to be?

Never	Sometimes	Half the Time	Often	Always

2. *What's Your State Of Mind?*

Your state of mind colors everything in your world, just like a pair of sunglasses. If your mind is at peace and happy it can be like looking through the proverbial rose colored glasses. Good things look beautiful and even awful things don't seem so bad. That happy peaceful feeling becomes the lens you use to interpret everything you see and feel. The same is true when you are stressed and upset. Like wearing dark shades indoors, that dark mindset can make even good things hard to see, and steal your sense of humor. That's why it's so important to keep an eye on your mindset.

Being in the zone includes being conscious of your state of mind and how it factors into your experience of things. It doesn't always mean you're in a great mood. Sometimes you've got to get good work done even on a crappy day. But it means you consciously deal with whatever mood you're in. What's more, you do what you can to have your mood work for you rather than being its victim. For example, if you know that you're in an angry mood, maybe you choose to do the physical part of a task rather than the part that takes calm, focused thought. Learning to be aware of and manage your own state of mind can be a valuable asset if you choose to develop that skill.

How Are You Doing?

How often do you feel in control of your state of mind? Where do you want to be?

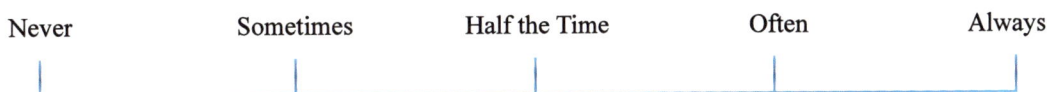

Never	Sometimes	Half the Time	Often	Always

3. Get Your Head In The Right Place...First!

If you are feeling anxious, upset, frustrated, lost, or desperate… stop. This is not the place from which to act. Take a few minutes (or longer if possible) to shift your state of mind, and get your head back into the right place.

What does that look like in practical terms? It often looks like what was discussed in the previous chapters. Slow down. Breathe. Connect to your Source, connect to yourself, and connect to others. This is an intentional action designed specifically to shift your state of mind, so that your actions can then be productive and even enjoyable.

How Are You Doing?

How often are you able to "get your head in the right place?" Where do you want to be?

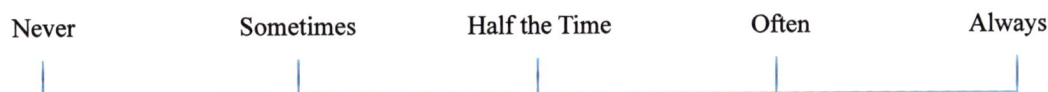

Never	Sometimes	Half the Time	Often	Always

4. Handle What Needs To Be Handled

Sometimes you need to take corrective action before you can move forward. For instance, if your head is in a bad place, there is usually a reason – it's important to handle that before you move on. If there is something upsetting you, one great way to move forward is to just deal with the problem.

If you are upset with someone, go tell them. If you are afraid of something, go do it. If you are worried about something, call a friend and get some support. Avoiding the issue generally makes things worse. Handling issues quickly is probably the hardest thing for most people to do, but also one of the most powerful.

How Are You Doing?
How often do you move quickly to resolve an issue? Where do you want to be?

Never	Sometimes	Half the Time	Often	Always

5. *Focus On Your Exactly Right Outcome*

I find that the best combo to move yourself forward is to be committed, but not attached. This means you know what you want to have happen, but you're not emotionally attached to how the outcome should look. You put 100% commitment to accomplishing your goal (as if your life depended on it), but your happiness is not dependent on the outcome of your efforts. This allows the creative force of the universe to work freely. Things can turn out better than you could of imagined, because you aren't limiting the outcome to what your imagination can create. It's important to keep an open mind.

Try using what is called Miracle Intent. "I'm intending a miracle. I have a basic idea of what I want to have happen, but I'm not attached. I'm really looking for the best possible outcome, even if I don't yet know what that is. Please help me notice it when it happens." And then get into action, making sure you keep that intention in the forefront of your mind. All kinds of great stuff can happen from this simple practice.

How Are You Doing?
How often do you keep yourself focused on your *Exactly Right* outcome? Where do you want to be?

Never	Sometimes	Half the Time	Often	Always

6. *Embed Yourself In A Group Of People Who Support You*

This is where your work from Chapter 8 comes into play. When you are going after your dreams, you will find from time to time you may slip, or be incapable of handling it on your own. That is normal. In these hard times the systems, structures and supportive people buttress you to keep things moving. With supportive people, you have a much better chance of staying on track.

How Are You Doing?
How often do you feel you're connected to supportive people? Where do you want to be?

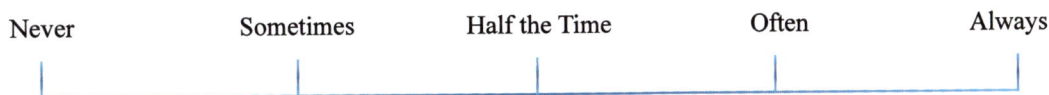

Never	Sometimes	Half the Time	Often	Always

7. *Keep Your Eye On The Mouse Hole*

As you practice these steps, it's important to keep your eye out for the blessings, gifts, miracles, and successes that happen along the way. Like a cat keenly watching for the mouse to appear from its hole, you keep your eye out for any evidence of success. It can slip by unnoticed like a mouse, since it's not always big and spectacular. But every success counts, and noticing one blessing may help you notice others. This is part of validating that your plan is working, and also a great way to encourage more success.

How Are You Doing?
How often do you notice and acknowledge blessings and successes that happen to you? Where do you want to be?

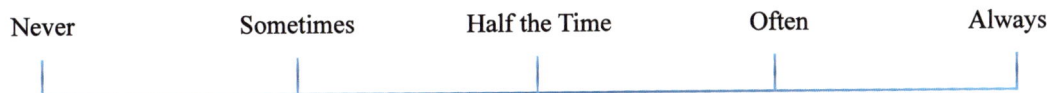

Never	Sometimes	Half the Time	Often	Always

Exercise 26:
Next Steps

Next Steps

All of these ingredients together create an amazing environment for Balanced Action. Please bear in mind, this process is not linear. It doesn't necessarily proceed neatly from step 1 to 2 to 3 and so on. Many of these steps will be in parallel operation as you live your dream. Often you may need to revisit several of them over and over throughout the process. They are merely steps which help you achieve the goals of your heart, and live your own *Exactly Right Life*.

1. When you look at your answers in the previous exercise, which area would you most like to improve? Look for the one that inspires you, or is the biggest bang for your buck. Jot it down.

2. What would improvement look like to you in that area?

3. Name one or two simple actions you can do to raise your score another level or two in the next month.

4. Name one thing you can stop doing in the next month that will help you raise your score.

5. Extra Credit: Take on a new area every month or two.

Get More Free Stuff

More is available!

Additional tools, articles, and recorded meditations have

been created to support your journey.

Check it out at:

www.MoveMountainsInitiative.com

on the Get More tab

GET MORE 9.1 Personal Warning Signs For Feeling

Out Of Balance

GET MORE 9.2 Ten Tips For Getting Your Head Back In The Game

GET MORE 9.3 Create Your Stop Doing List

GET MORE 9.4 Creating With Intention

My Thoughts

_____
_____
_____
_____
_____
_____
_____
_____
_____
_____
_____
_____
_____
_____
_____
_____
_____
_____

The Extraordinary

"The difference between ordinary and extraordinary is the 'extra'."

~Dr. Robert Anthony

Jump and make the leap into your own Exactly Right way of living. Trust that the net will appear. What's more, you may even find your wings and fly.

~Exactly Right Philosophy

Now What?

*I*f you have worked your way through to this chapter, then congratulations are in order. You've done some meaningful work. You've taken some important steps toward living the way you are designed – even if it doesn't seem like it yet.

In this chapter you will have an opportunity to look back and see the strides you have taken and the progress you have made. You will also look forward and decide where you want to go from here.

This chapter marks another point of choice on your path to your *Exactly Right Life*. Will you choose to have it be an end to your inquiry? Will you choose to have it be the jumping off point for a miraculous journey? Will you choose another route entirely?

Living an *Exactly Right Life* is, at its core, a choice. A choice about how to relate to the circumstances of your life; a choice to re-story those parts you want to change; a choice to let go and become free of past hurts; a choice to recognize the possibilities and little miracles all around you; and, perhaps most importantly, a choice of whether to feed your dreams or feed your fears. While you aren't in this life alone, how you choose to live it is primarily up to you. What will you choose?

✦ Let's Go! ✦

"Life loves to be taken by the lapel and told, 'I'm with you kid. Let's go.'"
~ Maya Angelou

Exercise 27:
How Does It Feel To Be You Now?

Where Are You Now?

Before you decide where you are going, it helps to know where you are and where you have come from. It's time to take a look at and acknowledge where you are and the ground you have taken to get here.

Look at the following set of questions that you answered in Chapter 1 of this workbook. Without referring back, assess where you are now in each of these areas. Put a check mark where you feel you are now. (Again, not where you think you should be.) Use the first response that comes to mind.

1. Are you clear about your passions?

Not at All	A Little	Halfway	Mostly	All the Way

2. Are you currently living your dreams?

Not at All	A Little	Halfway	Mostly	All the Way

3. Are you doing work that you love?

Not at All	A Little	Halfway	Mostly	All the Way

4. Are you spending time with people that encourage and lift you?

| Not at All | A Little | Halfway | Mostly | All the Way |

5. Do you feel energized and lively?

| Not at All | A Little | Halfway | Mostly | All the Way |

6. Do you live in an environment that nourishes and renews you?

| Not at All | A Little | Halfway | Mostly | All the Way |

7. Are you continually learning and growing?

| Not at All | A Little | Halfway | Mostly | All the Way |

8. Do you feel connected to Spirit?

| Not at All | A Little | Halfway | Mostly | All the Way |

9. Do you feel like you are living the *Exactly Right Life* for you?

| Not at All | A Little | Halfway | Mostly | All the Way |

Now, go back and look at your answers to these same questions from Exercise 1 and see your progress.

10. Where are you now in relation to where you started? Note the original check marks in Exercise 1. Having compared the two sets of answers, what stands out for you?

11. Where are you now in relation to where you wanted to be? Note the stars in Exercise 1. How do you feel about your progress?

Notice that it may be tempting to judge yourself harshly if you haven't made much progress in some areas. Don't give into the temptation. This is after all a process that can take a while. I encourage you to celebrate any successes you see and give yourself credit for a job well done. Making progress of any kind is a win. Even more so when it is progress toward living the life you were designed to live.

Where Do You Want To Go?

As you take time to look at how far you've come in this process, don't be too quick to rush on to planning the future. Give yourself permission to celebrate and enjoy all those things that have brought you closer to the life you dream of. Record them. Study them. Those things you have discovered, no matter how small, can be some of your best information. They provide powerful insight and guidance in helping you plan where you want to go next. They can help you make choices that will bring you more of the things you enjoy because you now have something to compare to. That is why spending time to recognize and celebrate the things you've already accomplished is so important.

Once armed with this guiding information – this real world feedback – then you can begin to chart your future course. As you do, keep referring to these insights to ensure that your journey is as enjoyable as your ultimate destination. Keep adding in those yummy *Exactly Right* experiences all along the way. After all, most of life happens in between the destinations, so why not enjoy the trip.

The next two exercises will assist you in integrating what you've learned about the unique *Design of You* and how you want to live your *Exactly Right Life* going forward. You'll have the opportunity to put together a "mini-plan" that includes action steps and the structural support needed to ensure success.

> "Dreams come a size too big so that we can grow into them."
>
> ~ Josie Bissett

Exercise 28:
Dream Board Check In

Let's revisit your Dream Board. Check in on your Vision that is reflected on the Dream Board in Exercise 6. Also, review the New Story you created in Exercise 12: Designing a New Story from the Heart. Look for three things:

1. What have you accomplished or made significant progress towards?

2. What important parts of your Vision, Dreams or New Story have you forgotten or let slide? Get reacquainted with those inspiring things you said you wanted for your life and recommit yourself to having them. How are you going to treat yourself to these things on a regular basis?

3. What things about your Vision, Dreams or New Story need to be updated or added to? After working through the exercises in this workbook, it is likely that your ideas of what you really want in life have gotten clearer. If so, this is a perfect time to update your Dream Board to reflect how you've grown so that it supports where you want to go now.

Exercise 29:
My Mini Plan

Once you've updated your Dream Board, I invite you to make a "mini-plan" for your future. A mini-plan is a short list of small supportive steps and actions that will keep you moving forward in your chosen direction – for now.

Why a mini-plan? It's early in the *Exactly Right* process. In my experience, this is potentially a time of significant change. If you commit yourself to a "Grand Plan" now, you might get bogged down with feelings of overwhelm. Or, you may feel locked into it, like you should stick with it, even when you're getting the message that it doesn't feel quite right for you.

Set yourself up to win from the beginning. Create a mini-plan to get into action – one that you have permission to play with and adjust as often and as radically as necessary. Be generous with yourself, and allow for unexpected growth. This is one of the key components in the process of designing an *Exactly Right Life*.

1. What are three main feelings / experiences that you want to integrate into your life now?

A.

B.

C.

2. For each feeling / experience list three actions or items that bring you that feeling or experience (or that you believe will do so based on what you have learned or imagined).

A.

    1.

    2.

    3.

B.

    1.

    2.

    3.

C.

    1.

    2.

    3.

3. What structures will you put in place to ensure that you take some of those actions or acquire some of those items? (Consider being detailed about times, dates, action steps, and the help you want to make this happen.)

Finally, give yourself a comfortable period of time to work your mini-plan. Maintain awareness of the plan by reviewing it on a regular basis to see how it's going. Tweak it as necessary to make it work for you. Consider posting the plan in your personal retreat space. This will help remind you to invite Spirit into the process.

Continuing The Journey

You now have the foundation you need to jump fully into the ongoing journey of discovery that's integral in living your *Exactly Right Life*. You have begun the climb that will lead you to the top of your own personal mountain! Perhaps you can already feel the movement that has taken place, the fundamental shifts - inside and out – that let you know you're well on your way. I am excited for you and invite you to continue approaching life with open arms. Your journey matters… Not only to you, but to the world. Like a sunrise over the peak of a mountain, your journey of awakening can bring beauty to the world.

We worked on Step One of Move Mountains Initiative in this workbook. It has been focused on giving you the foundation and the tools to harness your true power and enable you to move your personal mountain. It was designed to reacquaint you with your own miracle self and your natural connection to Source. Moving mountains takes realizing, committing, and fully using the best of yourself and your spiritual power source. It involves the whole of you, the human part and the spiritual part. Like climbing a real mountain, the further you climb toward the peak of understanding your Self, the closer you come to that point where the Heavens meet the Earth. Just like the mountain summit where the Earth meets the Sky, you will find that place within you where your Self and Spirit become one. Where you can "let go and let God" — living, loving, creating and contributing from the Heart of the divine.

> "Concerning all acts of initiative (and creation), there is one elementary truth that ignorance of which kills countless ideas and splendid plans: that the moment one definitely commits oneself, then Providence moves too."
>
> ~William H. Murray

What's next? Move Mountains Initiative is more than just your personal journey, though that's where it all begins. Ultimately, it's about the energy, power and miracles that are possible when individuals collectively embrace their "Big S Selves" and consciously share their gifts with the world. As we each find our place and weave ourselves into the greater tapestry, new and more wondrous vistas and opportunities will emerge for humanity. To assist in this unfolding, I have created a final audio visualization exercise to take you to that special place where the Earth meets the Heavens. Called the *Replenishing Your Soul Meditation,* it's a place for you to re-fuel with spirit-power. You can use this meditation again and again to revitalize your personal journey and gain insight to those opportunities and initiatives that have been waiting for you to come along. You can access this meditation and many other helpful resources at:

www.MoveMountainsInitiative.com
Click on the Get More tab

Thank you so much for taking the time to look deeply within yourself and see what more life has to offer – for you and for all of us. If you've gotten something valuable out of this work, please share it with others. What's more, I would personally love to hear about your triumphs. Please consider sharing them with me via email so I can post them on the website. Let's celebrate together as we journey to the mountain top.

Email Victories to:
Janet@MoveMountainsInitiative.com
Look for your story on the Victories Tab

It has been a privilege to share this work with you. May the love and joy you experience in living your passions and sharing your gifts be a beacon of light for all with whom you associate. Remember, the biggest gift you can give someone is the space to fully express their True Self and create their own *Exactly Right Life*. And in simply doing this, you will Move Mountains.

Get More Free Stuff

More is available!

Additional tools, articles, and recorded meditations have

been created to support your journey.

Check it out at:

www.MoveMountainsInitiative.com

on the Get More tab

For this chapter, look for:

10.1 Replenishing Your Soul Meditation

My Thoughts

_____

_____

_____

_____

_____

_____

_____

_____

_____

_____

_____

_____

_____

_____

_____

_____

_____

Wings to Fly

"When you come to the edge of all that you know, you must believe one of two things: There will be earth to stand on, or you will be given wings to fly."

~Author Unknown

Acknowledgments

I'm deeply grateful to my incredible writing team: Kevin Courington, Suzanne Tipton Offner, and Joan Prenger. They started all this with their clear intention and belief that they could create a life that was exactly right for each of them—and they wanted to share this with the world. Pick up a copy of their book: The Conversation Your Life Has Been Waiting For (www.ExactlyRightLife.com) to get the philosophy and process this Workbook is based upon. It fit like a glove with my personal philosophy and was my inspiration for the Workbook: I wanted an in-depth guide on how to apply the principles of creating the *Exactly Right Life* for me and others. For Move Mountains Initiative, it presented the perfect process for step one: harnessing our True Power to move our personal mountains, allowing our inner greatness to shine forth into our lives.

I hope you enjoy the journal-like format of the Workbook. Suzanne Tipton Offner was the layout genius and creative designer who made this happen. It couldn't have been done without her dedication and commitment, loving friendship, inspiration and just plain old hard work. Thank you from the bottom of my heart!

A special thanks to Kevin Courington for adding the spice to the written word when needed. I knew I could always count on him to add considerable value to the art of expression.

I would like to express an especially big thank you to my husband, Bill. Having been married over 25 years now, we've always allowed each other the space to pursue our passions. He has patiently supported me through this endeavor and I'm deeply grateful. Moreover, he contributed many of the peaceful photographs found in the Workbook.

I also want to express my appreciation and gratitude to Tessa Greenspan for connecting me to Suzanne Tipton Offner in the first place and ultimately, the *Exactly Right* team. A big thank you to Christine Evjen and Vicki Lenssen for their loving support and honest feedback as we spent a couple of months working through and testing the Workbook and applying it to our own lives. Vicki and I have been friends for over 25 years--the unconditional love, inspiration, encouragement, along with the best of times together, are priceless. I'm very grateful to Loren Ringer for early editing, guidance and continual encouragement. He inspires me to live life to the fullest.

To my friends and colleagues: Nikki Valenti, Alison Hendren, Robin Buck, Jody Barklage, Kay Kaiser and Mary Kay Sheets, thank you for your interest in this initiative and for taking the time to review the Workbook and share your wisdom and encouragement. You all hold very special energy from my standpoint and I feel extremely blessed that you have shared that with me.

Finally, thanks to our family in St. Charles, Missouri, who adds so much joy to our lives: Billy and Tuija, Sofia, Henri and Kalle; George and Christine, Camden and Tyler. Love you!

Janet Wittenauer

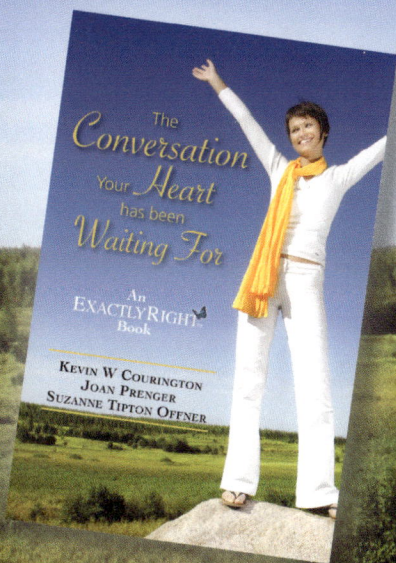

CPSIA information can be obtained
at www.ICGtesting.com
Printed in the USA
273191LV00008B